INTRODUCTION

In 1927 I found myself a lone pioneer missionary to Muslims. I longed for a textbook to give me some guidance concerning the evangelization of these difficult yet attractive people to whom God had called me. In the following forty-five years of active service among them, I learned many lessons, and some of these are passed on in this book. It has a twofold purpose: first, to help younger missionaries who feel called to work among Muslims in other lands; and second, to help the English-speaking person who wishes to know something more of the religion of those from abroad who now reside in his country. Although I have spoken to thousands of Muslims in several lands and have often seen them gripped with the message of the Gospel, it is not easy to instruct others in the art of winning them for Christ. The Muslim is proud of the fact that his religion is a worldwide brotherhood and that all Muslims are united. But, while the tenets of Islam do not vary, the language, background, customs and practices of each country differ immensely. The methods and lessons outlined in this book have been learned and taught in North Africa and in the Chad Republic. This book was originally written as a course in French and Arabic, and the colloquial Arabic words were also incorporated. Some of these words are included in parentheses and can be adapted to the lands to which the student hopes to proceed. The book is practical throughout and suggests how the various articles of faith and the practices of the Muslims can be used as the initial point of contact for the presentation of the Gospel.

Some lands dominated by Islam are closing to the Gospel, but many Muslims are moving to the Western countries. It is obviously the duty and privilege of every Christian to contact them with the Christian message. The Muslim is often bigoted, prej-

3

udiced, and fanatical, but he has a fear of God and is interested
in talking about religion. Muslims are approachable. It is not
impossible to win their confidence, and when contact is really
established they are often gripped with the Christian message.
Language plays a very important part. To be able to speak to
a man in his mother tongue is to reach his heart. This must be
the first aim of the specialist or full-time worker. For others it
will not be possible, and English will be the medium of approach.
Remember, then, that in English the Muslim's religious vocabulary will be very limited, and that words which have one meaning for you may convey something quite different to him. His
mind is not only prejudiced by the teaching of Islam but also by
the life, conversation, and beliefs of Westerners, all of whom he
regards as Christians.

SHARE YOUR FAITH WITH A MUSLIM

By

CHARLES R. MARSH

MOODY PRESS

CHICAGO

CONTENTS

© 1975 by
THE MOODY BIBLE INSTITUTE
OF CHICAGO

Fifth printing, 1980

Marsh, Charles R.
Share your faith with a Muslim.
1. Missions to Muslims.   I. Title
BV2625.M34   266' .023'0917671   75-15883

ISBN: 0-8024-7900-6

Printed in the United States of America

1

GENERAL PRINCIPLES

A careful comparison of John 3:1-21 with John 4:7-26 shows that the Lord Jesus presented the message to the woman of Samaria in a totally different way to that in which He confronted Nicodemus. In Acts 2:14-36 Peter proclaimed the Gospel to Jews, while in Acts 10:34-43 he gives virtually the same message to Gentiles. The message in each case is basically the same, but the presentation varies according to the background of the hearers. Different aspects of the same Lord are shown, using a different vocabulary and a varied appeal. Thus the people to whom we go must provide us with not only the vocabulary that we use but also the manner in which we present the unchanging message. It is not enough to know your Bible well; you must know the men to whom you go. The approach to a godless pagan is totally different to the way in which one speaks to a Muslim who believes in God.

There is also a wide variety in the culture, education and morality of Muslims. Some know the Koran well, while others can only repeat the first chapter. Some are really devout and God-fearing, while others make their religion a cloak for their sin. Every Muslim will bear the imprint of the land from which he comes, but the basis of his faith will be that of his fellow Muslims and in many ways the manner of approach will be the same.

On the other hand, many students from Muslim lands who are studying abroad will speak disdainfully of Islam, professing to have broken away from it while overseas. It is probable that the only way to really reach the hearts of such men is to speak their

5

native idiom well. The best way to approach them is as you would speak to agnostics of your own background. It will soon be seen how their profession belies the real state of their hearts and minds.

Again, some Muslims will be fanatical and bigoted, while others will be sympathetic and willing to listen. In the Western countries Muslims form a minority and for that reason may be suspicious of the motives of the Christian who endeavors to win their friendship. Yet here they are free from the general atmosphere of a Muslim land and can more easily break with the traditions and family ties which would otherwise keep them from accepting the Saviour. In every land the approach to men and women has to be different, just as the appeal to an educated Muslim differs from that to the illiterate. In dealing with the latter class in any land, the Christian must beware of instructing them in the religion of Islam as he discusses the relative merits of Christianity and Islam. Many a missionary to Muslims in Africa has unwittingly done this.

In many lands Muslims still have a very superficial knowledge of their religion. They repeat the witness to Muhammad, follow Muslim prayers, and observe the fast of Ramadān. Remember that while we should know what Muslims believe, our aim is not to compare religions but to lead them to a personal commitment to the Lord Jesus Christ as Saviour.

There is no doubt that a good knowledge of the vernacular and of Arabic, at least enough Arabic to know the religious terms important to Muslims, even when Arabic is not their mother tongue, is of primary importance in reaching Muslims abroad. They have their own religious vocabulary, and the Christian missionary must know and use it. This is not possible to the average person in the West or to the short-term worker. When we do use the English language to communicate, it is very important for us to help the Muslim understand the religious vocabulary that we employ. Such expressions as the atonement, Calvary, the cross, the new birth, regeneration, the Holy Spirit, and the Son of God either mean nothing to a Muslim or they may even convey a falsehood to his mind. In order that our message may be clear, such words should be avoided or explained. Our task is to convey the message to his mind in such a way that he will be able to understand and grasp it. In other words, we must communicate. Remember that the religious terms you use can be utterly meaningless to the person who is listening. On the other hand, even an Arabic word can have one meaning to the Christian and convey a totally different meaning to the Muslim mind. This was the disadvantage of many earlier missionary translations.

We may speak of heaven (*al janna*) and his thoughts turn to the Muslim paradise, a place where he will be able to satisfy his sensual desires with women who are perpetually virgins, a place of rivers of wine, etc. We must therefore seek to define heaven in other words, speaking of God's presence there, or of the Father's house. Prayer (*salāt*) to us is largely intercessory, but for the Muslim it primarily means the five periods for ritual prayer when he repeats the phrases which he has memorized. Prayer for him is primarily worship, or submission to the will of God, a mere form. When we desire to pray with him, we could suggest: "Shall we ask God's blessing (*barakat Allah*) on your home" or "on this sick child," rather than saying, "Let us pray together."

We shall often use the Arabic word believe (*āmana*), and by using this word every devout Muslim can honestly affirm that he does believe in the Lord Jesus. We must therefore show him the real meaning of faith by using other words which indicate clearly that saving faith involves the mind and belief in the historical facts recorded in the Bible (*Kalām* Allah). He must not only believe the statements and promises of the Bible, but implicitly trust (*ittakala*) the Lord Jesus for salvation, committing his life to Him and obeying His commands.

When we speak of sin (*danb*) he will probably think that we mean one or all of three things: adultery (*zina*), murder (*al qatl*), or the sin of associating a man with God, that is, of putting Jesus Christ in the place of God (*shirk*). To express various aspects of sin, he uses a wide range of words such as transgression, lawless-

ness, and disobedience. If we use these other words we shall
bring home to his conscience the true meaning of sin. An experienced worker among Muslims in the same land should be able to
supply the young missionary with such a vocabulary. It is of the
utmost importance to find the correct words in the vernacular,
and Arabic has a very wide religious vocabulary.

Some general principles should be used as guidelines in presenting the Gospel to Muslims:

1. *We should avoid condemning Islam or speaking in a deroga-
tory manner of the person of Muhammad.* Instead of criticizing
Islam, we should try to sympathetically understand it, putting
ourselves in the Muslim's place. It is wise never to allow oneself
to be drawn into a discussion of the life or character of the man
whom they honor as their prophet. Our aim should be to attract
him to the Lord Jesus, showing him that Christ is a living Person
who is able to save and who can satisfy his heart. The Lord gave
an important principle of teaching in His rules to the disciples
when He said, "Men do not gather figs from thorns, nor do they
pick grapes from a briar bush" (Lk 6:44, NASB). He inferred
that the thorns and brambles of controversy repel, but that everyone is attracted by fruit! To point out to a Muslim the deficiencies
of his religion is to antagonize him. Some Christians tell a
Muslim that Islam is a religion of works and that man can only
be saved by the grace of God. They will insist that the Muslim's
form of prayer is not true prayer at all, for God seeks a humble
and contrite heart and not the mere prostration of the body. They
will affirm that if Muhammad had been a true prophet he would
not have taken so many wives. The message of such Christians is
negative and critical. The Muslim is repelled, pricked by the
thorns. Our aim should rather be to present the true vine in such
a way that he may desire to gather for himself the fruit of the
Gospel. The presentation of truth should be positive. We do not
wish to provoke him to a retaliatory argument.

2. *We must remember that a Muslim is a believer in the one
true God and in His laws.* His ideas may be false, but a careful
study of the ninety-nine names of God that he repeats with the

help of his rosary shows that he believes in and worships the one true God, because many of these attributes are found in the Bible as well as in the Koran. Therefore one can always speak to him about God, His existence, power, judgments, faithfulness, and holiness. He knows that God is omnipresent, omnipotent, and omniscient. He should never be treated as a pagan, an agnostic, or an idolater.

3. *In the heart of every true Muslim there is a fear of God.* This is the strongest point in our approach. He not only believes in God theoretically, but he knows in the innermost part of his being that he must meet with God in judgment. He is aware of his own shortcomings and failures. He knows that there is a hell and is afraid lest he should be cast there. This attitude of fear is expressed when he prostrates himself in prayer, for he takes the attitude of a slave before his master. This is in direct contrast with the filial attitude of the believer in Christ who knows God as his heavenly Father; but where this true fear of God exists, it is the basis for an appeal to the conscience. The fear of God which is lacking in our own land today is still found in many Muslim lands. Men may explain it as superstition, but it certainly exists and every Christian worker among Muslims is aware of its value.

4. *Most Muslims have a certain sense of sin.* There is usually no deep conviction of sin, but the Muslim is deeply aware of his failure to attain the standard required by God. His religion does appeal to some extent to his conscience and to the Law of God which he knows he has transgressed. In his daily prayers he asks for forgiveness, and he continually repeats this formula: "I ask forgiveness of God" (*astaghfr* Allah). He knows when he has done wrong, and he hopes for forgiveness through the mercy of God. Yet, he is fully aware that through his religion he can have no assurance of forgiveness or pardon for sins. He can only hope. But the desire for forgiveness for sins exists deep down in his heart, and we can make use of this. He has little difficulty in understanding man's evil nature which the Bible refers to as the flesh or sin. Different men will express this in various ways, using

different words, but in every devout Muslim there is the acute awareness of evil within. He knows his nature is evil. He has a desire to do good but is unable to do so. He has sincerely tried to follow his moral code and failed. He knows that this is because of his own evil heart. Christ alone is the answer to his deep soul need. Let us bear this in mind in our approach.

5. *For the foregoing reasons we must try to forget that he is a Muslim and remember that he is a human being like ourselves and a sinner.* Sinners need a Saviour, and we alone have the message that can meet his need. As a Muslim he will seek to discuss his religion, appealing to the differences between Christianity and Islam. We must seek to bring him back continually to the realization of his need of a Saviour, trying to avoid discussion, and appealing primarily to his conscience rather than to his intellect. We must show him that our faith is logical. The whole man must be reached, theological problems must be dealt with, but the primary appeal must be to the heart and conscience.

One characteristic of a Muslim is that he is never ashamed to tell what he believes. He will always state his convictions quite plainly. Muslims will not hesitate to seek to get you to repeat the witness to Muhammad and to convert you to Islam. They admire this zeal and frankness—this open confession of faith—in others. No attempt should be made to hide the truths of the Bible, to tone them down, or to make them fit in with Muslim belief. Islam and Christianity are diametrically opposed, and it is impossible to seek a common faith by adapting the Christian message to Muslim thought. The Muslim has a keen perceptive mind and quickly detects any attempt to mask the truth or to compromise. Dr. Zwemer once said that you can say anything to a Muslim provided that you say it in love and with a smile. They respect the man who, alone in the midst of a crowd of Muslim opponents, has the courage of his convictions and does not hesitate to speak the whole truth. It is of the utmost importance that this outspoken conviction be backed up by a consistent life.

6. *It is also most important to remember that the message we bring is judged by the character of the messenger.* Indeed, at the

first approach the messenger is as important as the message. It is because in the past the messenger has so often been un-Christlike that Muslims and others have not wanted to listen to the message. The fruit of the Spirit is love, joy, peace, patience, kindness, goodness, faithfulness, gentleness, and self-control. These virtues together constitute a Christlike character, and they can only be reproduced in us by the Holy Spirit. The Bible everywhere teaches that it is the character of the servant that counts. The character that will count and be respected will be the love which goes on loving in spite of their hatred and bitterness, which suffers long and is kind, that bears all, believes all, hopes all things, endures all things; the joy in the Lord in spite of their opposition and persecution; the peace of God that they so earnestly covet; the plodding patience that continues to go on; the practical goodness which they cannot refute by argument; the faithfulness to one's pledged word; the man whom they know they can trust who has a living faith in God and His message to them; the meekness when confronted with their arrogance; and the self-control when tempted to blow one's top because of their senseless arguments. To this must be added a spirit of reverence and sobriety. Muslims cannot understand the lighthearted emotion that characterizes some Christians. A man of God is joyful, yet he must be sober and reverent, especially when he is speaking of the truths of God. Having stated all this, we can now affirm the most important principle in our approach and our teaching.

7. *We must make use of the truth that he knows to lead him on to accept the whole truth of the Word of God.* In this way we shall be able to find many points of contact as we explore what he believes and already knows. He knows that God is light and that in Him is no darkness at all. He knows that Christ is the Son of Mary. He is aware that one of His titles is the Word of God (*Kalimat* Allah). He knows that the Lord Jesus Christ will soon return to reign. He knows that a man must be pure to approach God in prayer. In this and in many other ways he has a glimmer of truth. We can thank God for this. We can congratulate him on what he knows and believes, and then go on to

try to lead him into deeper truth. He may not accept our teaching at once, but he will reflect. Let us then use the truth he knows to lead him into deeper truth.

8. *The next most important point to keep in mind is that the Muslim responds to love.* He must feel that we really care for him as a man, that we love him and have a genuine concern for *him,* and not only for his soul. In nearly every case of conversion of a Muslim, he has first been influenced by Christian love. Si Mebarek was a young Koranic student who taught the boys in the mosque to recite their holy book. For many years he had attended Sunday school classes, but the teaching had left no impression on him. He hardened his heart to the Gospel and mocked his teachers. When he was eighteen and very proud of his knowledge of Islam, he went to the home of a woman missionary and asked for a gospel in Arabic, saying he would very much like to read it again. The servant of God was thrilled. Here indeed was an answer to her prayers: a young man seeking the Lord. Si Mebarek took the gospel in his hand, glanced at it, and then with a look of defiance tore it to shreds and threw it on the ground, trampling on the pieces. He quite expected to receive a sharp reproof for having treated the Word of God thus. Instead he saw tears come into the eyes of the servant of God and, with a look of inexpressible sadness but of genuine love, she turned away without a word. She went into the house to pray for him.

Si Mebarek headed for home, but that expression of the patient love of Christ, of His meekness and gentleness, really reached his heart. Within an hour he was back again, now a convicted sinner seeking salvation. That simple expression of the love of Him who wept over Jerusalem effected what the years of teaching had failed to accomplish. The messenger is as important as the message.

This is where Christians have failed down the ages, especially from the time of the Crusades until now. Some missionaries still continue to battle against Islam with argument, abuse, and ridicule. It is so important to show this love in practical ways, gradually breaking down barriers. Never fail to greet your Muslim friend with a smile, even in times of political tension. Show sympathy in times of illness or bereavement. Render him little acts of service. Invite him to your house and accept an invitation to his. Be scrupulously honest in all business dealings. Show that you are a Christian in the smallest details of life. If a Muslim shopkeeper has given you the wrong change, be sure to point this out to him. Be respectful and show honor where honor is due. Show that you love him by trying to understand his point of view. Be a good listener. If there is one thing that God has taught me in my old age, it is the wisdom of patiently listening to the other person, be he an English teenager or a bigoted Muslim. If you can praise something that he says, by all means do so, but you must be transparently sincere. Muslims can read you like a book, and the nicknames that they often give various missionaries and others are always very apt. Remember that true love does not mask the truth. You have a message of love to communicate. Before the Muslim can accept it and love your Lord, he must learn to love you. Before he trusts your Lord, he must know that he can trust you. Remember, then, that love is God's way.

9. *Our closing emphasis must be on the work of the Holy Spirit.* We must depend wholly on Him to teach us what to say, to bring conviction of sin and faith in Christ, to create new life, and to give assurance of peace. Apart from this, all our efforts will be utterly futile (Jn 16:8-14).

2

ISLAM

Islam is the religion of the Muslims. The word implies surrender to God, for a Muslim is one who claims to be wholly submitted to the will of Allah. The expressions Muhammadanism and Muhammedan are distasteful to Muslims and should be avoided. The Muslims claim that Abraham was the first true Muslim, and the prophets who followed him were all true Muslims. This cannot be true in the sense in which the word Muslim today means one who believes in Muhammad as the prophet of God and is surrendered to the Koran as the will of God.

A number of books give the story of the life of Muhammad and the history of Islam, but it is not our purpose to write of these.

The religion of Islam consists in belief (*al īman*) and practice (*ad dīn*).

THE ARTICLES OF MUSLIM BELIEF

The Muslims believe in the following:

1. Allah who is unique, all-powerful, and merciful to all Muslims

2. His angels and evil spirits

3. His Scriptures, the "Revealed Books," of which there are four great ones: the Law of Moses (*Taurāh*), the Psalms of David (*Zabūr*), the Gospel of Jesus (*Injīl*), and the Koran of Muhammad

4. His messengers and prophets, of whom Muhammad is the last and the seal of the prophets

5. the day of resurrection

6. destiny, for whatever Allah decrees, either good or evil, must come to pass

THE PILLARS OF MUSLIM PRACTICE

The pillars of Muslim practice are five:

1. the witness (*shahāda*): "I witness that there is no God but Allah, and that Muhammad is the Messenger of Allah."

2. the ritual prayers (*ṣalāt*)

3. the paying of ritual alms (*zakāt*), to which can be added (*ṣadaqa*) voluntary offerings

4. the fast of Ramadan (*ṣaum*)

5. the pilgrimage to the Kaaba in Mecca for those who can afford it (*hajj*)

THE WITNESS

To repeat the words *"Lā illaha illa Allah, wa Mohammed Rasūl Allah"* is to become a Muslim. Although a person should repeat the witness with conviction (*nīya*), Muslims will rejoice if they can ever persuade a Christian to merely say the words. Thus, this is to be avoided. This creed is simple, easily learned and repeated, and the repetition of the formula incurs no obligation to any change in the moral life of the person who repeats it. To repeat the phrase is to become a member of the vast Muslim fraternity with the hope of ultimately attaining paradise.

Muslims will do all in their power to persuade a Christian to repeat their creed. What is to be the Christian's attitude to this, and how should he reply? "You must be aware that I cannot repeat your creed and say that I believe in Muhammad. I am a Christian. I am certainly a believer (*mūmin*), but I am not a Muslim. But I can bear witness (*ashahād*) to my Lord Jesus, and I should like to tell you just what difference He has made to my life."

It would be a good thing for the beginner to write out a short testimony to the saving power of the Lord Jesus Christ which he has experienced. Emphasis should be placed on three things: (1) What he was before he believed in Jesus Christ. (2) How he came to believe in Him. (3) The tangible difference that He has made in his life.

I always found it helpful to demonstrate my testimony in a practical way, for instance, by saying: "When I was young I loved the world with all its pleasures. I had been taught to follow my religion, to believe in God, to pray, to go to church (use the word for mosque), and to worship God. I was holding onto God with one hand and onto the world with the other. The attraction of the world was very great and I wanted to follow it, but I was afraid to go far into sin because I was holding onto God with my other hand. God pulled one way; sin pulled the other. There was a struggle in my heart; I had no peace. I did not dare let go of God, and I did not want to let go of the world. Then Jesus Christ came into my heart. He knocked at my heart's door, and I just said to Him, 'Please come in.' When He came in He took away the desire to sin. I let go of the world with its pleasures (*zahu*) and surrendered my whole being to God. Now that I am holding onto Jesus with both hands, the pain in my heart has been replaced by peace, and God draws me onward in His way." The words should be demonstrated by using one's hands.

Muslims will always listen to a testimony of God's dealings with an individual. It is something that they cannot contest or refute, especially when it is backed up by a pure, consistent life. Or again, the Christian can agree that God is one and tell of the man who came to Jesus Christ and asked Him which was the first and greatest commandment. Jesus replied, "HEAR, O ISRAEL; THE LORD OUR GOD IS ONE LORD; AND YOU SHALL LOVE THE LORD YOUR GOD WITH ALL YOUR HEART" (Mk 12:29-30, NASB). Certainly all Christians, Israelis, and Muslims will agree that there is only one God, but can anyone really say that he loves God with all his heart and with all his soul and with all his mind and with all his strength? It is so easy merely to assert a creed and forget the command that is implied: to love God. This could lead to an interesting discussion or talk about man's failure to love God and his need for a change of heart. Unless such a turn is made in the conversation, the Muslim will only want to discuss the failure of the Christian to accept Muhammad, because he accepts the first phrase of the witness but rejects the second.

PRAYER

Every devout Muslim performs the ritual prayers at least five times a day. These are the prayer of the morning (*al fajr*), at midday (*ad dh hur*), midway between midday and sunset (*al 'aser*), at sunset (*almeghreb*), and one hour after sunset (*al 'āsha*). These prayers are a ritual which must be performed in Arabic, and mainly express praise to God. Muslims are really sincere and reverent in their prayers. The prayer starts with the "formulation of intention": "O God, I intend to pray the morning prayer. . . ." Then follows the ceremonial purification when he washes the various parts of his body with pure water or, if this is unobtainable, with sand. He then says, "I witness that there is no other God than the one God, and that He has no partner, and I testify that Muhammad is His servant and His messenger. O God, make me the fellow of those who have repented and of those who are pure."

He then says, "God is great" and repeats the witness. He recites a short prayer, and then an invocation against Satan which he repeats three times, saying, "I seek refuge in God from Satan the stoned." He then repeats the first chapter of the Koran (*al Fatihah*), saying, "In the name of Allah, the Gracious, the Merciful. All praise belongs to Allah, Lord of all the worlds, the Gracious, the Merciful, Master of the Day of Judgment. Thee alone do we worship, and Thee alone do we implore for help. Guide us in the right path—the path of those on whom Thou hast bestowed Thy blessings, those who have not incurred Thy displeasure, and those who have not gone astray." He may now repeat part of the Koran.

He then says again, "God is great" and bows down. In this position he says three times, "Glory to God the Master of the worlds." He stands and says, "God hears those who praise Him." He prostrates himself three times while saying, "Glory to God the Lord most high." Kneeling, but lifting his head, he cries,

"God is great." Then he repeats this prayer: "O God, forgive me, have pity on me, and direct me, and preserve me, and make me great, strengthen my faith, and enrich me." Before bowing down a second time, he says, "God is great." Each prayer comprises a certain number of these *raka's,* according to the time of day. He now recites a chapter of his choice from the Koran and, if he wishes, he can say a short prayer of his own. He then turns his head to the right, to salute or greet the angel who is on his right, recording his good deeds, then he turns to his left to greet the angel on his left side who he believes records his bad deeds. He says, "Peace be unto you, and on you be peace."

Note the following points:

1. *The intention (an nīya).* What is the believer's aim in praying? Why does he pray? For the Muslim it is a duty (*wajib*), a precept or obligation (*fard*) and a debt due to God (*dīn*). For the Christian, prayer is speaking to his heavenly Father (Mt 6:5-15). But God cannot be your Father unless you have been born again. In John 3:1-14 Jesus tells us about the new birth. The one who believes in Jesus first listens to God speaking to him through the Bible, and then speaks to God in prayer. He knows that God understands every language, so he speaks to Him in his mother tongue. This aim or intention in prayer and faith is most important, and the subject can be developed. For instance, a Muslim can say that he believes in Jesus Christ, but a true believer believes in Jesus Christ with the intention of finding salvation in Him alone.

2. *The ceremonial washing.* The principle here is that a pure soul must speak to God in a pure body. So a Muslim must purify himself before each prayer. This is certainly a point of contact. It may well be that you have just observed a Muslim friend at his devotions or that he has deliberately chosen to pray in your presence when he is your guest. Instead of telling him that such prayer is unheard by God because it is a mere form or that mere pious phrases form part of a religion of works, why not take this line: "My friend, I noticed that before you prayed you carefully washed various parts of your body. I assume that this is because

you realize that you must be pure in order to approach a holy God. This is quite right, and the Bible says, 'Let us draw near with a sincere heart in full assurance of faith, having our hearts sprinkled clean from an evil conscience and our bodies washed with pure water' (Heb 10:22, NASB). Yes, you have grasped an important truth. To draw near to God you must be pure. I noticed that when you washed the various members of your body you neglected to wash your heart. You say that the heart is the king (*ṣultān*) of the members. Now if you wash the members of your body and leave the heart unclean, surely that is not enough. The motivating and controlling force of your body must be cleansed."

He will reply, "It is quite impossible for a man to wash his heart."

"Yes, I quite agree, but what is impossible to man is possible to God. The Word of God tells us that 'the blood of Jesus His Son cleanses us from all sin.' " (Read 1 Jn 1:7, NASB.)

You have praised the principle which is in accordance with the Word of God and have led him on to see that such bodily cleansing is not sufficient. He himself has admitted that he cannot purify his heart, and he may even ask you how man's heart can be cleansed. This is the principle: Start with the glimmer of truth which he has in his religion and lead him on to know the full revelation of God. Do not offend him by condemning outright his way of praying, but show sympathy and love, leading him on by the power of the Holy Spirit.

3. *The attitude of prayer*. The Muslim must bow down (*sajada* and *rak'a*) during his prayer, for he assumes the attitude of a slave before his master. This indicates a fear of God's wrath and punishment. It is in direct contrast to the reverence and holy boldness with which the Christian approaches his heavenly Father. It is possible to bow outwardly but to refuse God the obedience and submission of heart and life. Such Scriptures as Luke 18:9-14 and Acts 9:6 could well be used here.

4. *The opening chapter of the Koran can be used as a point of contact with better educated Muslims.*

There is a subtle difference between the two titles "gracious" (*ar Raḥ man*) and "merciful" (*ar Raḥīm*). The first word indicates what God is in Himself, and the second the goodness and mercy that He manifests in His dealings with men. How does God, who is eternally *ar Raḥ man,* show Himself as *ar Raḥīm* in forgiving love? The answer is to be found in the Christian faith alone. (See 2 Co 5:19; Jn 1:1-3, 14; 3:16.)

The opening phrases of the Koran, expressing praise to God, are continually on the lips of pious Muslims. "All praise belongs to Allah, Lord of all the worlds." The Muslim worships God as the Creator. The Christian also worships God as Creator but thanks Him for spiritual blessings. (Read Eph 1:3-9; 2 Co 9:15; Ps 103:1-6.)

"Guide us in the right path": this is an excellent prayer, but to be led in the right way we must know what that way is. Jesus Christ said, "I am the way" (Jn 14:6). It is not enough to know the way to your home; you must walk in it. Jesus will give you the life which will enable you to walk in God's way. Remember that God will not be pleased with you if you know that Jesus Christ is the way and refuse to follow Him. The prophets showed men a way to God, but Christ alone said, "I am *the* way."

5. *In his prayer the Muslim asks God for many of the spiritual blessings which are found in Christ alone.* For example, forgiveness of sins, refuge, guidance, preservation, peace, and salvation from Satan and his power. He confesses that he seeks a refuge in God. A refuge is useless if it is inaccessible. Christ is the Refuge and the Saviour (Heb 2:14-15; Ac 2:21).

6. *The most simple form of prayer for the Muslim is to invoke an attribute of God.* For instance, he will say, *"Ya al Ghaffā"* (Thou who dost pardon), and without expressing it he means, "O Thou who art ready to forgive, forgive me." When feeling his weakness, he will pray, "O Thou Mighty One" (*Ya al Qadīr*), implying, "Please strengthen me." He thus uses the attributes of God as a one-word prayer. This is calling on the name of the Lord and is only fully realized in Jesus Christ (Ac 2:21; Ro 10:14).

EXTEMPORANEOUS PRAYERS

In addition to the ritual prayers of Islam (*ṣalāt*) there are the prayers of intercession or petition (*du'ā*). In the former the worshiper bows down in the prescribed manner. In the latter he holds out his hands before him with the palms held upwards, as if expecting to receive a blessing from God. When praying for Muslims, or with them, it would seem permissible and natural to hold the hands out as they do, rather than in the normal Christian manner of holding the hands together and shutting the eyes. This surely is a small concession; and when one adopts this attitude and prays with Muslims in the name of the Lord Jesus, there will almost invariably be a responsive "*Amin*" at the end.

It is hard to see how Christians can possibly join Muslims in their ritual prayers since this involves the repetition of the *shahāda*, but every opportunity should be taken of praying in the presence of Muslims or, if at all possible, of praying with them. We must let them know that we pray regularly with our families and that we hold meetings for prayer to seek God's blessing on their land and their rulers. Before giving medical treatment in the home or at a clinic, the Christian should always pray in the name of Christ, using the prayer called *ad du'ā,* with his hands held out. In my clinic in Algeria I never treated the people without first praying with them, and without exception such prayer was followed reverently. The subsequent healing was then rightly attributed by the Muslim to the power of the Lord Jesus to heal and not to the skill of the missionary. This, in turn, prepared him to listen to a message from the Bible. The birth of a child, a visit to a sick man or woman, or a friendly visit are all occasions when one can say, "Would you like us now to ask God's blessing" (*barakat* Allah)? Thus, with a little holy ingenuity, the Muslim's fear of God expressed through prayer can be made an opening for presenting the Gospel.

3

THE FAST OF RAMADAN

The observance of the fast of Ramadān is an obligatory duty for all Muslims. They follow the lunar calendar, and the month of Ramadān is of twenty-nine or thirty days' duration. Every year it is approximately nine days earlier than the previous year. Each day's fast begins from the moment when one can distinguish between a white and black thread, and it lasts until sunset. The night is spent in eating and drinking, and more money is spent on food during this month than at any other time of the year. "How can we fast unless we eat well?" is a common comment. During the day it is forbidden to eat or drink, to smoke, swallow the saliva, to touch a person of the opposite sex, to play games of chance, and to have sexual relations. The nights are spent in pleasure and excess.

Children often start to fast for a few days when they are eight or nine years old, vying with each other to see who can keep it up for the longest period. A pregnant woman is permitted to break the fast if she feels her child is in danger. Women do not fast during their menstrual periods, but these days must be made up by fasting at some other time during the year. A traveler in the desert, a soldier engaged in the holy war (*jihad*), an old person who is very feeble, and children who have not attained the age of puberty are not compelled to fast.

The fast is a debt owed to God (*dīn*) and an obligation (*fard*). It is said to partly atone for one's sins, to help control the passions, and to merit a place in paradise. The Muslim must declare his intention to fast (*nīya*) before dawn each day. He is recommended not to swear or use vulgar language, not to lose his temper, or to speak evil of others during the fast.

Many Christians refer to this fast as the "feast" of Ramadān, and thus show their entire lack of sympathy for the suffering Muslims. The Christian worker should not give the impression that he also is fasting, but he will remember that these his fellow-men are suffering and thus will abstain from eating or drinking in front of them. They will often offer to prepare coffee or food for the evangelist during this month, but he should politely refuse, at the same time explaining his reasons. In many lands the law of apostasy in Islam is still applicable. This states that anyone who does not observe the fast is an infidel, whom to deprive of wealth and life is lawful. A female apostate is to be confined in a separate room, starved and beaten daily until she returns to the religion of Islam. The Christian missionary should remember that the convert who breaks the fast is in danger of being killed or poisoned. My book, *Too Hard for God?* * gives more information about this.

The Christian worker finds that Ramadān tends to disrupt the normal program of activities, and that during the fast the Muslims are inclined to be irritable and touchy. On the other hand, many of the men abstain from working at this time and are therefore free to chat. It is perhaps wiser to refrain from direct evangelistic effort during the first ten days or so. Later, people tend to get more used to the complete change of mealtimes. The women start preparing the evening meal (*fadhūr*) early in the afternoon, and Christian women workers must remember this. The last meal of the night is usually eaten about 2:00 A.M. and is called *sahūr*. It will be found that during Ramadān, conversation centers on fasting.

How should a Christian answer the Muslim if he asks him questions like these:

"Are you fasting (*ṣāim*) or eating (*fātar*)?" He could reply like this: "Tell me just what do you mean. Am I fasting from food or from sin? You know that the fast teaches self-control, and it is not only the desire to eat which must be controlled but all of

*See *Too Hard for God?* Published in 1970 by Echoes of Service, Bath, United Kingdom. Paperback.

man's carnal appetites. We Christians try to control our evil desires but find it impossible to do so without God's help. This is where a living Saviour helps us. Just as you control your desire to eat, you must control your eyes so that they do not look at wrong things or read filthy books. Keep your tongue from lying and slander. Control your hands and yourself (*nafs*) from all that is forbidden (*harām*). You will find that this is impossible in your own strength, and that is why you need the Saviour Jesus Christ."

If he should ask, "Did Jesus Christ fast or not?" read him Luke 4:1-2 and say, "Yes, He did abstain from food for forty days, but that was not during the month of Ramadān. He was not a Muslim. During that time He was tempted and found to be the perfect man. That is why He could redeem us."

"Why do you Christians not fast?" "Christians do fast. (Read Mt 6:16-18; 17:21; 1 Co 7:5; Ac 13:2.) But they do not fast during Ramadān. To understand why Christians do not observe Ramadān, you must remember why you fast (*nīya*). You fast so that God will forgive your sins. Christians already have God's forgiveness because Christ paid their debt. God has forgiven us by His mercy without our good works.

"The Jews asked the Lord Jesus why His disciples did not fast. His reply is recorded in Luke 5:34-38. Did He liken your Ramadān to a piece of a new garment put on an old garment? It is obvious that God cannot be satisfied with a month of fasting, good though it may be, when it is used to patch up a life of sin. The whole life must be renewed, and a new man must live in the new garment. Only Jesus Christ can do this (2 Co 5:17)."

The following are a few passages of Scripture that can be used to advantage during the fast. It should be fairly obvious how in each case they form the basis for a talk leading up to the question of salvation.

Isaiah 58:3-11. This is the true fast. Point out that during this month there are more quarrels and fights than at any other time of the year. Look at verse 4. Why did God not accept their fast? Because of their sin. The right way to fast is shown in verses 6-7, and the resultant blessings.

Mark 7:15-23. The Lord Jesus showed them that it is not eating food which defiles a man but what goes out from man's heart. Muslims will readily agree that the sins listed in verses 21 and 22 do defile and that man has need of cleansing. The sinful nature must be changed. Read John 3:1-7 and 1 John 1:7.

Acts 10:1-4. Cornelius was a good man who fasted and prayed, yet he lacked forgiveness. It was because he was sincere and feared God that God sent him messengers to show him how he could find forgiveness. Peter spoke to him of Christ, His perfect life (v. 38), His sufferings and death (v. 39), His resurrection (v. 40), and His return as Judge (v. 42). It was not until Cornelius believed in Christ that he found forgiveness (v. 43). Tell muslims that God has taken notice of their fasting and desire to please Him. He has sent you to them as His messengers to tell them just how they, too, may find forgiveness.

Matthew 6:16-18. Jesus taught His disciples that no one was to know when they fasted. Ask if it is not true that some Muslims are proud of the fact that they fast. They do not hide it. Ask them, "What is your intention (*nīya*) in fasting? Is it really to please men, or is it to win salvation by works?" (Read Ephesians 2:8.)

Luke 18:9-14. This parable of the Pharisee and the tax gatherer is perhaps the most useful Scripture for work among Muslims during the fast. The application is obvious.

Much wisdom, love, and patience as well as tact must be exercised at this time of the year. Some missionaries have tried to show love and sympathy for the Muslims by fasting with them during Ramadān, but without the intention of thereby gaining merit. But this has not been understood and has not really helped win any Muslims for Christ.

4

THE RELIGIOUS FEAST OF 'ID

The fast of Ramadān terminates with three days of rejoicing (*'īd al Fitr*). Seventy days later there is the feast of *'īd al Kabîr* or *'īd al Adha.* Every family slays an animal, preferably a ram with very large horns. They recall that God sent a ram to Abraham to be killed in the place of his son. Muslims insist that it was Isma il (Ishmael) who was placed on the altar, not Isḥaq (Isaac). It is interesting to see that the idea of sacrifice (*dahīya*) exists in Islam and that there is also the teaching of a man being redeemed (*fada*) by an animal. This feast is always a time of great rejoicing, but a number of problems confront the Christian who is in touch with Muslims.

The Muslim will often invite his friends to eat with him at this festival or will bring him some of the meat of the ram that has been killed. Should Christians eat this, or will it compromise their faith? If the Christian worker refuses to eat, will the Muslim be offended? It is probable that in different Muslim lands the answer will not be the same. Let us bear in mind the following points:

1. Many poorer people will wish to show their gratitude for some service rendered by the missionary during the year. This is almost the only time when they are able to offer something which they value, and many do wish to show their love and appreciation in this way.

2. To refuse to share a meal or to decline to accept a gift can be a real barrier. To eat with any people, sharing their food, sitting with them and obviously enjoying their company, is the quickest way to their hearts.

3. In all Muslim lands any meat that is sold in the market has been killed by the Muslim butcher who will pronounce the Muslim formula and turn toward Mecca in the same way that every Muslim does when he slays the sheep at 'īd.

4. Some weak Christians may regard the eating of such meat as participating in the Muslim faith, and this may cause them to stumble. It may even be that some Muslims take the same view. But where the Christian refuses to pronounce the *shahāda* or to observe the month of Ramadān, this is extremely unlikely. It is the weak Christian who is most likely to object.

5. By inquiry and by listening, the Christian should ascertain just what significance is attached to the shedding of the animal's blood. In some lands it is regarded as a sort of atonement for sins or as a magic power to protect from Satan, demons, and unseen powers. Each worker among Muslims must decide for himself, bearing in mind such Scriptures as Romans 14:1-23 and 1 Corinthians 8:1-13. Each one must be fully persuaded in his own mind before God, remembering the impression that his action will make, first on the Muslims, and then on any weak Christians. If a Christian does decide to refuse to accept the meat killed at 'īd, or to partake of such at a meal, he should do so very politely, apologizing profusely, and explaining his reasons. It is best to explain before the occasion arises, and not in the presence of others so that your Muslim friend will not feel embarrassed.

This festival is an excellent opportunity for presenting the Gospel by means of the story of Genesis 22:1-13. Be very careful to speak of Isaac as Abraham's son, as this will avoid needless discussion. They will always add the name Isma il, but it is absurd to spend time in discussing the fact that it was Isaac. When he is converted the Muslim will be prepared to recognize the truth of the Bible, and until that time minor points like this must be subordinated to the one important aim of leading him to personal faith in Jesus Christ.

Read Genesis 22; John 1:29, and Hebrews 10:1-18 or parts of these Scriptures. Illiterate or semiliterate people will be unable to concentrate while you read long passages of Scripture. Pick out the essential verses, learn the rest by heart, and be able to almost recite the story by memory. The main points are:

1. *The boy was condemned to death,* but blissfully he was ignorant of his danger. God had told Abraham to take his son and to offer him on the altar. God's judgment rested on him. He left home in the morning in high spirits. He was going to spend the day out with his dad and was very happy. He did not know that he had been condemned to death by God. God told Abraham to put some stones together, to place wood on them, to bind his son, and then to slay him, afterward burning his body. (Muslims will not know what a burnt offering is.) That boy was like men and women today. They are under the judgment of God, condemned to die, and yet blissfully ignorant of it (Ro 3:19-20).

2. *He was awakened to the truth.* He reflected that the people of that land often offered their children in sacrifice on the mountains. Suddenly he realized the truth, and one question was uppermost in his mind: "Where is the lamb?" He understood that if there were no lamb for a sacrifice he would be killed. This is the solemn truth. *Every man must bring a sacrifice or become a sacrifice.* Consequently, down the ages this heartrending appeal has sounded: Where is the lamb? Where is the lamb sufficient to redeem man? It is obvious that the animal that is sacrificed at the festival of 'īd will not suffice. It was bought in the market for a price, and man is beyond price. How much is the youngest boy worth? He is invaluable. He is precious because he is God's creation, made in the image of God. Therefore he cannot be redeemed by the blood of an animal (Heb 10:4). It is impossible that the blood of bulls and goats should take away sin. When any soul is awakened to see his danger, he will seek someone to save him, a lamb to redeem him. Where is the lamb?

3. *He was saved.* Praise God for that. God sent a ram so that the boy should not die. *But Abraham did not see it.* He was a true believer who had surrendered everything to God. He believed that even if he sacrificed his son, God could raise him from the dead. He was fully surrendered (Muslim) to God, but he was

blind to the most important thing. God had sent the sacrifice. His son need not die, but Abraham just could not see it until God in His mercy sent a messenger to show him. (Read Gen 22:11-13.) You, dear friends, are just like Abraham. You just cannot see that God has sent a Lamb to die for you. John the Baptist (*Yaḥya ibn Zakaria*) saw Jesus and said, "Behold, the Lamb of God who takes away the sin of the world!" (Jn 1:29, NASB). We have come to show you that Jesus is the Lamb of God's provision. God sent Him to be the one all-sufficient sacrifice for the sins of the whole world. You are like Abraham. You believe, you claim to be fully surrendered to God, but until now you cannot see the essential truth that Jesus is God's Lamb. That is why we have come to you. Listen, I will read John 1:29. (Then tell the story of the crucifixion very simply.)

Abraham unbound his son and let him go free. Then he offered the ram in the place of his son. Listen to the lad as he praises God: "Praise God, I am saved! I am free! God has saved me!" If an Arab had heard him, he would have said, "Be quiet, lad, don't say 'Praise God, I am saved.' We can only say '*In sha Allah* (or *Ma sha Allah* I shall be saved.)' " The lad turns to his father and says, "Dad, is it true that you will kill me as well as the ram?" Abraham replies, "No, son, God has redeemed you. God sent the ram. You are safe."

Then the boy could say, "Praise God, I am saved!" Likewise, the Christian can say, Praise God, I am saved; for God will not demand a payment twice, first at my bleeding Surety's hand, and then again at mine. (Read Ro 8:1; Jn 3:16-18.) The lad did not say, "Thank you, Dad, for buying a ram," but "Praise God," because God provided the sacrifice, etc. It should be obvious that this theme can be developed and it is one of the simplest yet most impressive ways of putting over the Gospel truth to a Muslim by starting with what he already knows. So keep these three points in mind: condemned, awakened, saved.

5

ISLAMIC BELIEF

The Muslim believes in Allah who is unique, all-powerful, and merciful to all Muslims.

ALLAH

HIS ONENESS

This is their dominant thought about God and is expressed in the phrase "*Lā illaha illa* Allah" (There is no God but Allah). He is absolutely unique and inconceivable by man. "Whatever your mind may think of, God is not that." This idea utterly excludes the thought of the holy Trinity. The greatest sin that man can commit is to worship anything else but Allah or to associate any other being on the same level with Him.

HIS GREATNESS

Allah *akbar* (God is great, or more literally, God is greater) is constantly repeated in Muslim prayers. God is far greater than any thought that man can have of Him. Because of His might and power, the Muslim bows in worship, taking the attitude of a slave. Allah is so great that He can do what He likes, even break His own laws. The word *al Qāder* not only expresses His might, but that whatever God decides will take place. It is useless to try and struggle against what He has decreed. From this comes the word *mektoub* (it is decreed or written). Everything that happens in the world is decreed by God, and in Islam, man's free will is practically eliminated.

HIS MERCY

Allah *ar Raḥ mān wa ar Raḥīm* (God is gracious and merciful). He will have pity on all Muslims even though they sin, but He does not love all men. It is very hard for the Muslim to think of God as our Father. He suspects that this would mean a physical fatherhood. He finds it very difficult to understand the love of God as expressed in Jesus Christ. In fact, some former Muslims who are Christians would insist that this is the very last line of approach to Muslims.

Many pious Muslims carry a rosary which has ninety-nine beads, each one standing for a name of God. The one-hundredth name is ineffable and is unknown to men. Many maintain that the camel alone knows it, and that is why he has such a proud look because he alone possesses this knowledge. It will be obvious in our talks with Muslims that it is not necessary to insist that God exists, as when one first approaches pagans. It is important to seek to communicate a correct idea of God who is love, light, and spirit. We shall ever need to remember that man cannot know God as Father except by a direct revelation (Mt 11:25-27). Once more we are reminded of our dependence on the Spirit of God.

Our line of approach will vary according to the mentality of the Muslim. With a modern man who has been trained to think and who has had contact with Christians, we could compare the theology of the Bible with the Koran:

In Islam God sends, but in the Bible God comes Himself. In Islam God sends His prophets and messengers. He sends books, etc. In Christianity God became man. The Word was made flesh (Jn 1:14). God was in Christ reconciling the world to Himself (2 Co 5:19).

In Islam man is committed to seek after God who can never really be found. In the Bible God seeks man and finds him (Lk 19:10; 1 Ti 1:15). The parables of the lost sheep and lost coin (Lk 15:1-32).

Islam is one of the world's religions, and in every religion that which is stressed is what man must do for God. Man must work for salvation. He must pray, go to the holy place or the mosque.

The Gospel message tells of what God has done for man. His work is always perfect. "It is finished."

In Islam man takes the initiative; he must seek God. In the Bible God takes the initiative. He chooses, calls, seeks, saves, and the Holy Spirit convicts of sin, shows man his need, and reveals Christ.

In Islam man tries to earn life by observing a series of prohibitions and taboos: "Do this." "Don't do that." The New Testament tells of a new life that God gives to man. Man dies to live. Having received new life through the death and resurrection of Christ, He loves God and wants to please Him.

The parable of the prodigal son always appeals to Muslims (Lk 15:11-32). The Christian should learn to tell it in a realistic way, putting in local color. The father still loved his son even though he was in the far country and doing wrong. When the son returned, three possibilities lay open to the father: (1) He could have given up the son entirely. This attitude would have been unworthy of a loving God. (2) He could have beaten him severely when he returned and refused to have received him. How unlike God! (3) He could have continued to love him, to patiently wait and suffer. In such a situation, who is it that suffers most: the father or the son? This suffering opened the way for the son to come back (1 Pe 3:18).

It is sometimes useful to compare God's love and His justice. Use both hands, the right hand signifying God's justice and the left His mercy. If He had acted in judgment and condemned all men to hell, He would have been just but would have gone against His character as a loving God. If He had shown mercy to all men without requiring repentance and taken all men to heaven, He would have been loving but unjust, and heaven would be similar to this world with all its sin and suffering. He must be equitable (*al 'adil*). Hold both hands together with the palms up. How can He show His mercy and love and yet be just? If His justice is stronger than His love, that is not right. If His love is shown at the expense of His justice, that cannot be right. The only answer is to be found in the Gospel message (2 Co 5:21;

Ro 3:23-26). (Illustrations taken from human life do not help the sophisticated Muslim, but they are often of use with simpler people.) The worker among Muslims will often use 1 Timothy 2:5 when they insist upon the oneness of God: "One God, and one mediator."

6

ADDITIONAL ISLAMIC BELIEFS

THE HOLY BOOKS

Muslims maintain that God sent down 104 books and of these there are four important Scriptures: the Law of Moses (*Taurāh*), the Psalms of David (*Zabūr*), the Gospel of Jesus (*Injīl*) and the Koran of Muhammad. The latter is sometimes called *al Furqān*. The Koran is the last and the greatest and annuls all the others. Muslims assert that the true *injīl* has been lost and that the present gospels have been changed to suit Christian doctrine. Present-day Islam is founded on tradition (*al Hadith*) as much as on the Koran.

Should a Christian quote from the Koran in order to convince his hearers? This would seem inadvisable for several reasons: (1) The Bible is the sword of the Spirit, and to put this aside to quote the Koran is to turn from divine power to human reasoning. (2) Muslims will not accept teaching on their Koran as authoritative when given by a Christian. (3) They will insist that the Christian who uses the Koran to support his teaching should be consistent and accept every part of that book. The missionary to Muslims should certainly have a knowledge of the Koran, and would do well to learn some key verses by heart, but the Scriptures are authoritative and powerful. We should give great prominence to the Bible in our dealings with Muslims. We must not only quote the Bible, but read from it in their presence. The Koran calls Christians "the People of the Book" (*ahl al Kitāb*). A Christian is not considered to be a heathen (*kāfir*) or an idolater. What better name for us than this: "The People of the Book"? Let us then be the people of the Book. Read it

34

aloud to them, expound it, appeal to it, answer their objections from it, and place it in their hands. Do not be content with merely quoting it, but read it, especially if you can read Arabic.

All Muslims believe that we have changed the Word of God to bolster up our false doctrines. They will watch us carefully to see if there is any evidence of this in our teaching. When reading a passage, we must never attempt to compromise and to skip a verse which is controversial. They know that we believe in the deity of Christ, His atoning death, and risen power. To seek to avoid these truths when reading to Muslims from the Bible is to convey the impression that we are cowardly and that we do not really believe the Bible to be the Word of God. Let us be the people of the Book. I spent over thirty-five years in evangelizing the Muslims of Algeria. For the last twenty years of that time it was no uncommon experience to go into a coffeehouse where men would be playing cards and gambling. These Muslim men would often put down their dominoes and cards and ask "Sheikh, read to us from The Book." Sick people who had waited for treatment for several hours because of the crowds would insist that a message be given them from "The Book." This surely is proof that the Bible is the inspired Word of God. It can grip a hostile fanatical audience and transform them into eager, silent listeners. We *must* use the Book.

THE PROPHETS (AL ANBĪYA WA AR RUSŪL)

Many Muslims will assert that God sent 124,000 prophets and apostles, and that there are three great prophets: Moses, Jesus, and Muhammad. Muhammad is the last and the greatest; he is the seal of the prophets (*khātim*). Muslims will be able to tell the names of about thirty prophets who are found in their Koran: Harūn (Aaron), Ibrahīm (Abraham), Adam, Dawud (David), Alisa' (Elisha), 'Uzair (Esdras), Isḥaq (Isaac), Isma il (Ishmael), Ya'qūb (Jacob), Yaḥya (John), 'Isa (Jesus, in the Koran; in the Gospel, called *Yasū*'), 'Ayyūb (Job), Yūnus (Jonas), Lōt, Maryam (Mary), Mūsa, (Moses), Nōḥ (Noah), Suliman (Solomon), Ṭalut (Saul?), Zakaria (Zacharias), Chu'aib, Idrīs

(Enoch), 'Amrān, Jalut wa Ṭalut (Saul and Goliath). Also Dū al Kifl, Hūd, Sālih, Dū al Qurnain (Alexander). They prefix each name with a title: Sayyidna Ya'qūb (our lord Jacob).

In the Koran all of the biblical accounts have been changed and falsified. When speaking of them, it is not necessary to point out the errors, but to simply state the truth as found in the Bible. The very fact that they know the name of the prophet will make a point of contact and the story will interest them, for instance, the account of the Creation or the Deluge. The following are all useful passages that the student should mark in his Bible: "all the prophets" (Ac 10:43; Lk 24:25-44); *Lalla Maryam* (the title "lady" is always prefixed to Mary the mother of our Lord, Lk 1:26-38; 2:4-14); Yaḥya ben Zakaria (John the Baptist) and the message of repentance which he brought (Lk 3:2-17); Nōḥ (Lk 17:26-27); Mūsa (Lk 9:28-36); Ibrahīm (Lk 16:19-31; 13:28).

An Illustration

This apt illustration was given by an old Christian man who had been converted from Islam. It is the sort of illustration (*mathal*) that they really understand. He said, "O Abd al Masiḥ, every prophet is like the moon which shines in the darkness of this world. A prophet will be born like the new moon, and he will increase in size and power until he is like the full moon, then he will decrease and die. But do not worry. God will not leave the world in darkness, for another moon will be born. That is like the prophets; they were sent one after the other. A prophet came, gave his message, and died. But look at that sun, Abd al Masiḥ, and tell me if it is the same sun as you have in your country. Have you ever seen it decrease in size or strength? Jesus said, 'I am the light of the world.' He is like the sun. He is for all mankind, for every race, and He will never decrease or die. Abd al Masiḥ, look up into the sky. Can you see the moon? Of course not, for the sun is shining and who needs the moon when the sun has come?" The lesson is even more appropriate and forceful in view of the symbols on every mosque.

THE DAY OF JUDGMENT

The Muslim thinks often of a coming day of judgment. It is called *yaum ad dīn* (the day when debts will be paid, i.e., when man shall give an account to God), *yaum al qiyāma* and *yaum al ba'th* (the day of resurrection), *yaum al ḥisāb* (the day of reckoning), *yaum al fasl* (the day of division), and *yaum al akhir* (the last day). They believe that God will take a balance and will weigh the good and evil deeds of each person. If the good deeds outweigh the bad, the man will be saved. If his sins outweigh his good works, he will go to hell. But God is great and merciful to all Muslims. He will forgive those whom He wills to forgive. The decision on that day will depend on His will and not on His justice. Muhammad will be the great intercessor and will intercede (*shafi'*) in favor of all Muslims. Or again, all that a man does is written in a book, and on the last day the books will be opened, and his account will be placed in his right or left hand. If it is put into his right hand, he will be saved. If in his left, he will be lost. Salvation is according to works. What a mixture of truth and error.

Use the truth that the Muslim knows about a future judgment to teach him the whole truth from the New Testament. What did the Lord teach about judgment? (Jn 3:14-21).

HOW WILL GOD JUDGE?

"This is the judgment that light is come" (Jn 3:19, NASB). God first enlightens man about himself and his sin, and then about the only Saviour and about the conditions of salvation. Man is condemned already. God loves him and has sent salvation; each one must accept or reject it.

WHY DOES GOD JUDGE MEN?

Because they turn from the light they have because their deeds are evil. They love darkness rather than light (v. 19).

WHEN DOES GOD JUDGE?

Here and now (v. 18). There are two classes already: the

condemned and the saved. No need to wait. Men's works show
in which class they are (vv. 20-21).

"God sent the light through Jesus Christ by the Bible, His
Word, through us, His messengers. *We have brought you the
light.* The light has come to you." The other points of Muslim
belief are often relevant. Their belief in angels, good and bad,
their fear of every form of evil spirits, all show an interest in the
unseen world over which in the gospels the Lord Jesus is seen to
be Lord and Master.

Angels and Evil Spirits

The fear of evil spirits plays a very prominent part in the lives
of many Muslims. This belief is not only founded on the Koran,
but antedates Islam, being a part of African pagan religions that
has been incorporated into their religion. They believe that the
whole universe and every part of it is occupied with good and bad
spirits, or jinn. If a Muslim enters an empty room, he will greet
the spirits and say, "Peace be upon you." When he meets a
fellow Muslim, he does not say "Peace be upon *thee*" but uses
the plural, greeting not the man, but the accompanying angels or
spirits. At other times he uses this expression of greeting to de-
termine whether the person he is addressing is also a Muslim. The
person's answer will indicate whether he is.

Evil spirits are said to lurk especially around cemeteries, and
in empty houses, or in the proximity of water, blood, or ashes.

In many parts of North Africa the high places once devoted to
Baal worship still remain, and the names of the mountains are
alternately male and female. In Algeria, until the war for independence, animals were sacrificed on the mountaintops to the
"gods of the country" in times of drought. On such occasions
large companies of men and women would spend the night together on the high places, feasting and sinning. It is impossible
to enter the small buildings which are erected on the summit of
the mountains without being aware of the presence of evil. How-
ever, it must be stressed that this fear of evil spirits is a part of the
culture in which the Muslim lives, rather than an actual part of

Islam itself, that is, what Islam actually teaches, even though some Muslims have incorporated it into their belief.

Many Muslims wear charms or amulets around their necks or on their bodies. These *al ḥurūz* contain verses of the Koran, cowry shells, seeds, etc., and are said to protect the wearer from every sort of evil influence. The hand of Fatima is often seen painted on the walls of Muslim homes. A mother will place a knife under her baby's pillow, and hang a small silver hand round its neck to protect it from the "evil eye." A jealous neighbor will enter the room, look at the child with the evil eye, and leave. The next day the child refuses to eat, gradually wilts, and eventually dies. On one occasion my wife took our very pretty little girl to a Muslim wedding party. A friendly woman approached her and said, "You had better take Saliha home at once. They are looking at her and talking about her." She did so at once, but that night the perfectly healthy child developed a high fever and became really ill. Prayer in the name of the Lord Jesus was the only remedy.

Sometimes Muslims will attempt to hinder God's work by placing charms in a missionary's house, by tying up plants in the yard, or by placing a tangled mass of string near a door through which inquirers pass. They will also attempt to use drugs or magic on the converts and the workers. It is important to be forewarned of all these things, and the fact that the missionary is aware of them makes his approach to the Muslims much easier. "They are beginning to know us" will be their reaction.

It will not be long before the worker among Muslims encounters one of their "holy" men or women. These people foretell the future by means of wheat, sand, or barley; they often fall into a frenzy and speak unintelligible gibberish of an ecstatic language. Most of them are mediums and their influence is wholly evil, separating husband and wife, bringing discord into a happy family, keeping a Christian from fellowship, etc. It is only fair to say that many modern teachers in Islam condemn all such superstitious practices. A determined effort was made in Algeria at the time of independence to stamp them out, but the average

Muslim still retains a very real fear of the spirit world. He does believe in Satan and often uses the formula *"bi ism* Allah" (in the name of God) to shelter him from the influence of evil spirits. Again, this is part of the culture of the area where the Muslim lives and not true Islamic belief.

The lesson for Christian workers is twofold. We must always remember that we are fighting a spiritual foe (Eph 6:11-12). This must cast us on God. A Christian walking with God, sheltered under the precious blood of Christ, and empowered by the Holy Spirit, need not fear the effect of charms or talismans or demons. Our young children must be dedicated to God and committed to His safe-keeping. They should be taught proper behavior for visiting a Muslim home and guided in their relationships with Muslim children. Jesus Christ is Lord of the spirit world, and part of the Gospel message is to proclaim His victory over Satan and all his hosts. The Koranic version of the Fall of man, in which Satan plays a leading part, is utterly false, but the Muslim will listen reverently to the biblical account; this can serve as a preparation for and an introduction to the Gospel message.

The accounts of Christ's power over evil spirits are very relevant. Matthew 8:28-34; 9:32-33; and 12:22-29 are a few examples. Faith in His name triumphs over evil spirits, and the Christian has no need of amulets or charms.

Increasing contact with uneducated Muslims will reveal the extent to which their lives are influenced by fear of the unseen world or dominated by evil spirits, but the believer would do well to beware of seeing the occult in everything. Walking in communion with God, by the power of the Holy Spirit, he will be able to demonstrate in a practical way that Christ has entered the strong man's house, has conquered Satan, and in His name every form of evil can be encountered and overcome (Mt 10:1; Mk 16:17).

7

THE LORD JESUS CHRIST

Every Muslim professes to believe in Jesus, but it is "another Jesus." The 'Isa of the Koran is only one prophet among 124,000. He was sent only to the Jews. He was not the Son of God. He denied the Trinity. He was born of the virgin Mary, but Gabriel was his father, according to Bedâwî.* While still a small baby he spoke, and when he was a child he made a clay bird and caused it to live and fly. He was created of the dust as was Adam. He healed the blind and cleansed the lepers and had power to raise the dead, but this was only by God's permission. He foretold the coming of Muhammad (see Jn 14:16). He cursed Israel. He was not crucified and did not die; it only seemed so to men. He lives today and will return to this earth where he will marry, have children, and die at Medina where he will be buried in a prepared grave beside that of Muhammad. He will reign for forty years and will establish Islam in the whole world.

Is this 'Isa our glorious Lord, or another Jesus? Some would suggest that by substituting the name Yasū' for 'Isa we can present the true picture. Experience shows that the change of name effects little. We must put the correct content into the word and in this way communicate the truth. This can only be done by our teaching, our preaching, and our conversation. Whichever name is used by Christians in the country to which the new worker goes, he should never speak of Ennebi 'Isa or 'Isa al Masih, but always give Jesus His title of Lord. This will be *Rabbana* or *Sayyidna*. Many Arab Christians working among Muslims prefer

*Bedâwi was a Koranic interpreter in A.D. 1282 who wrote many books on Islamic theology.

41

to speak of Him as *Sayyidna al Fādi* (Our Lord the Redeemer)
or *Sayyidna al Masiḥ* (Our Lord Christ).

We must now face the fact that the Koran categorically denies
the two outstanding truths of the Gospel: the deity of Christ and
His atoning death. The greatest possible care should be taken
by the Christian when he refers to Jesus as the Son of God; otherwise he will communicate a lie while faithfully insisting on the
truth. Attempt to understand the Muslim viewpoint. He believes that the term "Son of God" means that God had sexual
intercourse with a woman, and Jesus was born as a result. This,
they say, would be blasphemy. God is great. When He wants to
do anything He has only to say, "Be" and it is done. Muslims
recite Sura 112 of the Koran in their prayers. This says, "Qul
huwa Allahu ahad . . . Lam yalid wa lam yūlad" (He is Allah,
the One, He begets not nor is He begotten.) Muslims really feel
that the name Son of God is dishonoring to God and to the Lord
Jesus. Yet, many really do want to know the truth about the
person of the Lord Jesus, and some are prepared to consider that
the term can be used in a spiritual sense.

We must somehow communicate the fact that Jesus is divine,
for a Saviour who is less than God is a bridge broken at the far
end. Yet, to tell a Muslim that Jesus is God is to widen the gap.
He will ask if we mean that when Jesus was born, then God was
born and when He died, God died. With considerable scorn he
will ask who was looking after the world when God was dead for
three days.

COMMUNICATING THE TRUTH CONCERNING THE SON OF GOD

1. Let us consider how one can avoid communicating a lie
through insisting on the truth. When the Muslim asks, "Was
Jesus the Son of God?" we must never give an unqualified affirm-
ative reply. Rather, respond, "What do you understand by the
term *Ibn* Allah?"

He will probably reply, "It can have only one meaning, and
that is that God went to bed with a woman and a baby was born."
He has stated the lie in his mind. Now you must kill it.

"No Christian in all the world believes that. It is absolute blasphemy. We Christians would not dare express such a thought."

In astonishment, the Muslim may say, "Then what does it mean?" We must then be prepared to communicate the truth.

2. Let us remember that Muslims accuse us of making a man God. We must remind them that we never attempt to do this. The Bible teaches that God became man. The eternal Word became flesh. The movement is from above and goes downward, not from below moving up. This can be illustrated by arrows pointing up and down and supported by Scriptures such as John 1:1-18 and Philippians 2.

3. The Pharisees often asked Jesus if He was the Messiah, but He seldom said, "Yes, I am." Why was this? Simply because their ideas of the Messiah were false. He conveyed the truth about Himself in other ways, for instance, by taking the name of God and adding to it simple illustrations such as "I am the bread of life, I am the good shepherd, and I am the door." We also must try to convey to the Muslim something of the wonder of the person of our Lord without using the term "Son of God" until he has begun to understand. Let us remember that until he grasps this truth he cannot be saved (Jn 3:36). It will take time to really communicate, but when one has done so, how very rewarding it will be. (See the study in the next chapter.)

4. It will appear to many sincere Christians that to refrain from speaking of Jesus as the Son of God will be to tone down the truth and to be unfaithful. But a careful study of the messages given by the apostles in Acts will reveal that when speaking to pagans or non-Jews, they did not refer to Jesus as the Son of God but used the expression Lord. The text of Acts 8:37 rests on manuscripts of doubtful authority. In Acts 9:20 and 13:33 the message was given to Jews. In other places where the Gospel is proclaimed to non-Jews, the Lord Jesus is referred to as "the Lord." When people believed in Jesus, they were then led on to a fuller understanding of His eternal Sonship as seen in the epistles. If our message is to be effectively communicated to the

people to whom we go, then they must provide us with the vocabulary that we use.

5. It would seem that the Arabic word *Rabb* (Lord) conveys the thought of One who is supreme, for it is used continually by the Muslims of God. Let us speak then of *Rabba na 'Isa,* our Lord Jesus, thus clearly implying His deity.

6. The first step is to assure our Muslim friends that we only believe in one God and not three. Many of them think that Christians believe in God the Father, Mary the mother of God, and Jesus the Son. We must insist that Mary was only a woman and that Jesus was born by the power of God without a man.

7. We can explain that in everyday speech the expression "son of" is used as a metaphor (*mathal*) and does not imply a physical relationship. For instance *ibn al ḥarām* means a bad man. This could be followed by "the son of a jackal," or "sons of thunder." We do not think of a jackal having human babies, or of the thunder bearing children. The term merely conveys the thought of likeness.

8. A study of the use of the word in the gospels does a lot to convey the true meaning. Just go through these passages: Luke 1:35; 3:22; 4:41; 8:28; 9:35.

9. The Muslim often refers to Jesus Christ as *Kalimat* Allah (The Word of God). We can read to the Muslim John 1:1-4, 14, and say "God does speak to men. He speaks through His Word, as I do. Where were my words before they came from my mouth? In my brain or in my thoughts; but if you cut open my head you could not find them there. In some mysterious way I and my word are the same. Whatever my word does, either by pleasing you or annoying you, you can say that *I* am doing it. So whatever the Word of God does, God Himself is doing it.

10. When we read, "In the beginning was the Word. . . . All things were made by him," etc., the Muslim will listen, and we are then starting to communicate. Let us rely on the Holy Spirit to reveal to the Muslim the beauties and glories of our Lord.

8

JESUS THE SON OF GOD

This chapter contains a nearly complete outline of an address that I first gave in a village in the mountains of Algeria. The only European in the district, I was spending a fortnight among the Muslims, sleeping in a disused coffeehouse entirely at their mercy. Each evening between twenty and thirty Kabyle men gathered to listen to my message. I had spent much time and prayer in preparing this address, and the first evening I gave it in fear and trembling. I knew the violent reactions of fanatical men to the truth of God. After the meeting the men filed out in silence, but did not disperse. Then one of them returned.

This is it, I thought, *they have come to kill me.* To my surprise, the man said, "Thank you so much, Sheikh, for that message. It is exactly what we want to know. We do want to know who Jesus Christ is. Tell us more tomorrow, more about Him." He left and five men came in, one after the other, to express their appreciation.

Months later I spoke to Arabs near Algiers on the same theme, and the response was the same. Later still, I used it in the desert in yet another dialect. It is the only message which has been so deeply appreciated by a Muslim audience that several men have returned to say thank you. Obviously some points are lost in English, especially where Muslim terms are involved. Perhaps it will be suggestive of similar talks. It can either be used as an address, or one or two points can be discussed with an individual on successive evenings. Let us make much of Christ.

WHAT DO YOU THINK OF CHRIST? *(Mt 22:42).*

What do you think of Christ? Everything depends on the answer which you give to this question: your happiness in this life, and where you will spend the life to come. Soon Jesus Christ will return, and when He does so He will ask you as He asked the Pharisees of old, "What is *your* opinion of Me?"

I come to you today as a Christian. I want to be your friend. I really want you to know who Jesus is, and it is most important that no one should mislead you about this important matter. Please do not think that He is just a prophet, a good man, one among many. No, He is unique, He is incomparable. There is no one like Him in this world or the next.

WHAT DO YOU THINK OF HIS WONDERFUL BIRTH?

No other was ever born as He was. He is Jesus the son of Mary. You call Ishmael the son of Abraham, John the son of Zacharias, Muhammad the son of Abdullah. All other men take the name of their father. Why did Jesus take His mother's name? Because He had no earthly father. He was born of the virgin Mary. He was born by the power of God (*qudrat* Allah) apart from the intervention of a man. Seven hundred years before He was born, the prophet Isaiah foretold how He would be born (Is 7:14) and it happened exactly as it was foretold, as you can read in Matthew 1:18-25.

God created Adam our father from clay, and all of us are children of Adam and so were all the prophets. We are of the earth, earthy. The Lord Jesus came down from heaven. He is called *al Manzūl*: He who descended. He was pure and clean like the snow and rain. All others are like the earth: dirty, impure, and tainted with sin. We read that "Christ Jesus came into the world to save sinners" (1 Ti 1:15). He came to a foreign place, just as I came to your country. You did not come to this place. You were born here. Jesus was in God's presence before He came. He chose to come to this world to save us. "In the beginning was the Word." (Read Jn 1:1-3, 14). He took a human body and became man. He came from above.

Two men once fell into a deep pit. One said to the other, "Save me from this wretched place. Please get me out of the dirt and mud." The other replied: "You idiot, how can I? I am in the same plight as you." They were both in the pit, and neither one could help the other. Then they heard a voice from above calling to them to grasp a rope. The man who had not fallen into the pit was the only one who could save them. He brought help from above. The very best man among the prophets could not save us from the pit of sin, but Jesus did not inherit a sinful nature. He came from above. God sent angels to announce His birth (read Mt 1:20 and Lk 2:9). How wonderful all this is. Never man was born as this man. He is unique in His birth. He is incomparable.

WHAT DO YOU THINK OF HIS CHARACTER?

He was perfect. He never once sinned. He never made a mistake. He never had to ask forgiveness (*astaghafr*). Every man who fears God must confess his sin and ask forgiveness. David did. Abraham did. In fact one prophet said that he asked forgiveness of God seventy times a day (This was Muhammad, but do not mention his name). You can search the Bible and the Koran in vain to find a single verse where Jesus asked forgiveness. He did not need pardon for He was sinless. His closest companions wrote about Him and said, "He knew no sin. He did no sin. There was no sin in Him." They were men who knew Him well. God forgave the prophets when they confessed their sin, but Jesus needed no forgiveness. He was without sin. He could even say to His enemies: "Which of *you* can silence me by pointing out one sin that I have done?" (Jn 8:46, Arabic). Not one of them could point to a single sin in His life. Who of us would dare to make such a challenge to our enemies? Jesus was brought before the judge Pilate and falsely accused, but Pilate could find nothing wrong, so he washed his hands and said, "I am innocent of the blood of this just person." There was never another man who was sinless. He is the only sinless Prophet. He is unique and incomparable.

WHAT DO YOU THINK OF HIS WORDS?

On one occasion His enemies sent the police to arrest Him. They listened to His teaching and then came back without having arrested Him, saying in amazement: "Never did a man speak the way this man speaks" (Jn 7:46, NASB). Think of what He said. He said: "I am the light of the world; he who follows Me shall not walk in the darkness, but shall have the light of life" (Jn 8:12, NASB). An old man once explained to me what Jesus meant. He said: "You know, friend, the prophets are like the moon. The moon shines in the night, and the prophets brought God's light to this poor dark world. The crescent moon is just like a prophet. It shines more and more until it is full moon, and then wanes and dies. But never fear. Another moon (month) will come in its place. So the prophets came one after the other. One gave his message, died, passed on, and left his place to another. Every nation has had some light from God. Men's religions are like the light of a candle or the moon. But who uses these lesser lights when the sun has risen? Jesus said: "I am the light of the world." He is the sun of righteousness. Have you ever seen the sun wane or grow less? No, it never dies; it is for everyone in every land. Jesus Christ is like the sun. He never grows less. He is for every land, for every man. He also said: "I am the way, the truth, and the life." Now the prophets all came to point the way back to God. They said: "This is God's way. Do this. Follow this teaching. This is the way. Keep the commandments." But Jesus said: "I *am* the way. Follow me."

A small boy lost his way in a big city. He was from another land and was unable to express himself clearly. He asked a policeman to tell him the way home. The policeman said to him: "Go up this street, take the second turning on the left, then the third on the right, cross the bridge, go around the roundabout, and up the middle road—" The boy burst into tears. The policeman had told him the right way, but the boy was too weak and fearful to follow the instructions. Just then a man

ing to famine and misery, and the narrow way which brought him back to the plenty of the father's house. Or again the lesson of Luke 16:19-31, showing two men in this world who became separated by the great chasm.

THE WORDLESS BOOK

This is the next best subject for beginners, and it can be used with individuals as well as groups. It might be well to remember that with Muslims, heaven is always thought of as green, not golden, and that hell fire is black. A clean handkerchief can be used to cover the black page and illustrate the good works which do not take away sins, but only *cover* them. The man appears to be clean until on the Day of Judgment God removes the good works and reveals the sinful heart. The place of good works is located after faith in Christ, which brings cleansing. Then when the good works are examined on the Day of Judgment, they are found to cover a pure heart. A number of local proverbs can usually be found to bring home the truths of this and other lessons. Local proverbs must never be used to replace the Word of God, but they can often be used to put over truth in a few words. I collected over 500 Kabyle proverbs in Algeria. "Good works take away sins" is obviously not true, but it can be changed to "sins ruin good works." "You who are clean and shining outside, what is your inward state?" Hunt up suitable proverbs, making sure of the exact meaning they convey to the people, and use them.

THE GULF BRIDGED

This is the title of an illustrated tract which is published by the Stirling Tract Depot in Classical Arabic. It is most useful. The white page illustrates a holy God. The next page is black and shows man in his sin. The third page shows a black chasm that is sin which separates man from God. The fourth page shows men with various planks with which they hope to bridge the gulf, and the last page shows the chasm bridged by the Lord Jesus Christ. A long strip with "faith" printed on it, is placed on the bridge and reaches from side to side. The same subject can be used with flannelgraph and outlined as follows:

1. *The gulf made.* Man was created to enjoy the presence of God, but he sinned and was driven out of Eden (Ro 5:12). Make two sides to the gulf, one white, bearing the word Allah, and the other black, bearing the word "man."

2. *The gulf bridged by Christ at Calvary.* (1 Pe 3:18; Eph 2:13.) Make short strips of cardboard bearing these words: good works, prayer, fast, etc. These fail to bridge the gap. Then a red strip "by His blood" and another of equal length, bearing the word "faith." This is placed over the word blood.

3. *The gulf fixed.* (Lk 16:26.) It will be too late to change after death. This makes a most impressive subject. It is perhaps too aggressive for a first approach, but Muslims really do admire the man who knows what he believes and says so plainly.

FORGIVENESS OF SINS

This is a subject to which one returns constantly, especially if treatment is given to sick people in their homes or at a clinic. Luke 5:17-26 is the text to be used. Here are the points to make:

1. *A sick man.* What's wrong? He wants to walk but cannot. (See Ro 7:19.)

2. *Worthwhile friends.* They know someone who can heal him, and they bring the man to Jesus. That is our aim, for we are your friends.

3. *An almighty Saviour.* He can heal the body and save the soul.

4. *People who hindered.* The crowd came between him and the Lord. This also happens today.

5. *A hard word.* "Son, your sins." Jesus knew them all. He knows *your* sins.

6. *A gracious word.* "Your sins are forgiven." He is able to bring forgiveness, for He died for sins, the Righteous for the unrighteous, that He might bring us to God. He is the one Mediator.

7. *Critical priests.* They were ignorant of His power for they did not believe in Him.

8. *A striking proof.* "Rise," new life; "Take up your bed," new strength; "walk," new walk. He found both healing and forgiveness.

JUDGMENT

Many Muslims are deeply concerned about the Day of Judgment, and over the years the following message has been a great help.

Prepare to meet your God (Amos 4:12; read Jn 5:1-14, 24). God has given us this world so that we may prepare for eternity. You must die, you must pass into eternity, you must meet God. But how will you die? How will God deal with you, as a Judge or a Father? In eternity there are two places, heaven and hell. Where are you going? The prophet told us to prepare, but he did not tell us how. Jesus did. He said: Listen to My word, believe me, and those who do find three tremendous blessings.

There was a crippled man who had not been able to walk for thirty-eight years. He longed to be cured. Every day he was carried to the baths, hoping to be cured. Every day he said, "*In sha* Allah, I shall get better today," but he never did get better. How like you. (Read Ro 7:19-20.) Jesus said: "Listen to My word."

1. *A word about his will.* Do you want to be healed? (Give teaching on repentance.) Do you want to be the man God wants you to be? To be made whole? God wants to save you (1 Ti 2:4). The devil wants to destroy you. You stand between them. If you really desire it, Christ will heal you. God has given you a will to decide, to choose between good and evil. The man replied, "Sir, I have no man. I cannot. . . ." Looking at Jesus, he must have thought, "Only You can help me." His trust was in the almighty Saviour, not in many prophets.

2. *A word about his faith.* "Arise, take up your pallet, and walk" (Jn 5:8, NASB). You cannot, but I can: "Arise." He

gave him new life: "Take up your pallet." He gave him new
strength: "Walk." He made him a new man (2 Co 5:17). This
is the miracle that takes place in every heart that trusts the Lord
Jesus. The man was immediately criticized, and you will be too.
They thought in terms of religion. He obeyed his newfound Lord
(Jn 5:10-11).

3. *A word about his conscience.* "Sin no more!" (v. 14). See
1 John 3:4-9. He found three blessings (Jn 5:24):

a) He passed from death to life (conversion).

b) He possessed God's life, a new life (new life in Christ).

c) He was saved from the coming judgment.

Many other outlines could be given. Those given above have
been used, and God has blessed them to the salvation of some.

12

OUTREACH TO WOMEN AND GIRLS

A tremendous gulf exists between the Muslim girl studying at a European university and her illiterate sister who spends her life shut away in a hovel in North Africa, or between the affluent veiled woman living in a city and her unveiled amoral counterpart in Central Africa who walks miles to a country market to sell her butter and cheese. It is this wide range of social distinction, degrees of literacy, divergent local customs in different countries, etc., which makes it very difficult to give guidelines on this subject.

Perhaps in the majority of cases three things characterize all these women. First is their background of fear, for this is the controlling element in their lives. From early childhood a girl's brothers are encouraged to beat her and to dominate her life. As a child she is taught the power of evil spirits, and talismans and charms are hung around her neck. When married, the fear of divorce hangs over her head like the sword of Damocles. She fears her autocratic mother-in-law who controls the household. When young, the mother-in-law had been made to suffer, so she will see to it that her daughter-in-law suffers as much, or more, than she did. When there is a co-wife, each is afraid that the other woman will plot against her so that her husband will turn her out. She is afraid of the gossiping tongues of the old women who go from house to house spreading trouble, separating husband and wife. When her baby is born, she fears the neighbors who may come in and covet it and then bewitch it with the evil eye. Above all, there is the fear of death and the hereafter, for many believe that women have no place in heaven although

Islam teaches that women and men both have an equal possibility of going to paradise. But of course neither men nor women can be sure if they will go to paradise. All Muslims have the fear of the hereafter, and the woman shows this fear even in her devotions. It is fear that makes her pray, that compels her to fast and to witness to Muhammad. She bows down to Allah and takes the abject position of a slave prostrating herself before a hard master. For the girls and women who do trust the Lord Jesus, there is the same continual fear of evil tongues, of threatened divorce, of poisoning or drugs, of whippings or beatings, and of every form of ill treatment. Because of this inbred tendency to fear, she sometimes doubts the sincerity of her fellow believers and fears that by their malicious or idle talk they may cause her persecution.

The second characteristic of Muslim womanhood is that they are dominated by men or by a single man. Many modern girls would be unwilling to admit this, but it is a fact. Islamic law teaches that a woman is a half person in the matter of inheritance, and that her husband has complete authority over her. Father and brothers keep a close eye on their daughters and sisters. The married woman is under the heel of her husband and would not dare to do anything or go anywhere without his permission. To attempt to do so would be to court divorce. The divorced woman or widow is closely watched by male relatives. The immoral conditions that prevail in many Muslim lands make all this necessary, but this situation affects any attempt to reach them with the Gospel or to help them when they become Christians.

Whatever the outward veneer due to Western influence, there is always an underlying superstitious awe of the unseen spirit world, a respect for the religious leaders of Islam, and usually a deeply ingrained fear of God. Much of this may be hidden from the Western missionary who is unable to speak her language fluently, but it forms the background of her life and may form the chief line of approach to her heart.

The woman missionary who wishes to reach these women must first of all realize that she herself knows nothing about her job—

yes, nothing. Bible school training, Western methods of mass evangelism, outreach techniques, and the feeling that "We are *the* people, and you just must listen to us" must all be persistently put aside, for such attitudes not only repel but can do untold harm. Observation over more than fifty years has shown that this is probably the hardest lesson for the missionary to learn, but it is absolutely essential.

The principles that Paul lays down in his epistle to the Galatians are as applicable for work among Muslim women as in any other type of Gospel work. Let us try and learn from him.

His Aim

"Until Christ be formed in you" (Gal 4:19). This was Paul's ardent desire, and it must be ours: not to preach to them, not to persuade them to change their religion or merely to believe in Jesus Christ, but that new life be formed in them by the power of the Spirit of God. Whatever line of approach we may take, whether it be teaching them to read, teaching them to speak a European language, caring for their sick, distributing literature, or following up correspondence courses, our aim must always be the same: that Christ be formed in them. Christianity is not merely a religious message which they must believe, but a *life* to be received in the person of the Lord Jesus. His life must be reproduced in the lives of Muslim women and girls. Therefore, a profession of faith, whether made orally or on paper, is not enough; there must be new life, and this will be evident in changed conduct. Here *we* can do nothing. Christ can only be formed in them by the new birth brought about by the power of the Holy Spirit. It is not our work for God, but His work through us. "My little children," writes Paul, "I am perplexed about you" (Gal 4:20, NASB). "Are you my children or are you really children of God?" He pinpoints the danger in Muslim work. They may get to love the missionary, to imitate the worker, to become her children, to rely on her. And then when the missionary withdraws, they feel that they are orphans, quit attending the Christian gatherings, and backslide. How often this has happened in Muslim work. Yet, on the other hand, these women must to some extent, first become the missionary's children. They must learn to trust her before they learn to trust her Saviour. They must love her before they love Him.

HIS APPEAL

"I beseech you, be as I am" (Gal 4:12). This was always Paul's appeal. When he stood before Agrippa he could say, "I would to God, that . . . not only you, but also all who hear me this day, might become such as I am, except for these chains" (Ac 26:29, NASB). Not a prisoner but a Christian. "Christ is so real to me that I want you to share with me His life, the joy and peace that He alone gives, the assurance of forgiveness and salvation. Become as I am."

This must be your appeal, and you can only say it as Christ lives in you. More than this, you must say it by your life. Paul radiated Christ and so must we. He could not be hidden. This is what Muslim women and girls must see: Christ in you and in me. Therefore, in your approach, you the messenger are of equal importance with the message. The value of your message is conveyed by your character, your conduct, and the manner in which the message is given. Your personal experiences, your whole attitude, and your life are an integral part of the Gospel. The Muslims instinctively know if you love them or if you just are condescending to go to them as a duty that you must perform.

HIS APPROACH

This is threefold. First, "I also have become as you are" (Gal 4:12, NASB). Paul put himself in their place. This is a most important principle if we are to communicate. They must realize that you love them enough to share. You must be prepared to sit with them, to listen to them, to sympathize with them, until they really understand that you do care and want to get to know them. I often had occasion to do this when I traveled from village to village in the mountains of Algeria. I would ford the mountain torrents, sometimes be soaked to the skin in the drenching rain, then sit with them on their mats around a smoky fire and share their frugal meal. The smoke that stung their eyes stung mine until tears poured down my face. The fleas that bit them bit me. I shared their hard mat for a bed and breathed the smell of the animal manure, as the cows and sheep shared the same room. This is the way to really understand them, to sympathize with them, and to really get to know them, to find out how they feel, think, and react.

It is not enough to know your Bible. You must know the women to whom you go. If you really want those women to become like you in faith and doctrine, you must first become like them through love and compassion. This is God's way. He became man in order to speak to men. He spoke our language, bore our trials, and faced our temptations so that He knew men by experience. He sat with the woman at the well. He let her talk. He used everyday language that she could understand and word pictures that she could grasp. He got down to the hard facts of her life. If you want to win Muslim women for the Lord, it is essential that you learn their language and learn it well. It is in learning their language that you learn to know them.

There are three stages in learning a language. In the first stage you learn to convey the message in words to your friend. In the second you are able to understand all that she says to you when talking on any subject, and in the third stage you can grasp all the little "asides" between her and the other women. You even understand their sign language, as they speak with their eyes or their toes. This must be your aim. *Then* you will reach their hearts. You will soon find that the women have a language of their own, which even the men do not fully understand. But you must learn it.

If you do not do this, you will find that even though you are convinced that you have faithfully spoken the truth and put over a message, in reality you have communicated a lie. So you must share yourself and not just your message. It will mean giving up precious time to listen, to share their problems, to weep with them, to sympathize, to show them that you too are weak and failing, but that you know of One who is able to help and sustain. Until they have accepted you, they will not accept the message you take to them. Remember that it may take years before you are accepted.

A young woman went to a large French town to contact Muslim women. She was able to rent a cheap flat in a large block of flats where she was the only European. The population of that city was cosmopolitan, and it was a cesspool of crime. Fellow missionaries pointed out to her the danger of living in such a place. "The surroundings are filthy, the din is continual, the building is unsanitary, your life will be in danger." She persisted and within a few weeks she had over ninety Muslim children coming to seven Bible classes. Young women visited her, she was friendly with the neighbors, and before long she was accepted as one of them. The missionaries in their large comfortable homes, away from the filth and the noise, wondered at her success. But her success was due to the fact that she followed the principles laid down by Paul.

Then, having put himself in their place, Paul did not hesitate to tell them truths that they disliked. "Have I therefore become your enemy by telling you the truth?" (Gal 4:16, NASB), he asks them. He was outspoken, bold, and fearless. He came with the authority of a living Lord, and to this they responded. His method was in direct contrast with that of the false teachers. "They eagerly seek you," he says in verse 17 (NASB). "They pander to you, and adapt their message to your desires." In direct contrast, Paul told them the truth.

To put yourself in the place of a Muslim woman does not mean that you tone down the message for fear of offending her. If you are prepared to stand for the truth with Muslims, they will respect you, be they men or women. In Algeria a group of teenage girls from Muslim homes were discussing the church that they attended on Sundays. "We go week after week, but there is nothing that wounds us, nothing that pierces us, nothing that really hurts." In astonishment a servant of Christ, Abd alMasih, asked, "But surely you do not want to be wounded?" "Of course we do," they answered, "for if we are not wounded we shall never come to Christ to heal us." How very true. The sister of one of these girls, a young woman of eighteen, said, "We have never met a servant of God who loves us so much. That is why he is such a help, and can say to us things that no one else ever dared to say."

A young Muslim man came to the house of a woman missionary while her husband was away. He suggested that he should come in and wait until her husband returned, but she refused. "But you are a foreigner and that is what people do in your country," he said. She replied, "I am living in Iran. I have neighbors, and I am sorry that I cannot let you in." How right she was. Was the young man offended because she did that which was right? On the contrary, both he and the neighbors admired and respected her. Such action goes a long way in gaining the respect, love, and confidence of the people. They will say, "Here is a God-fearing woman, a woman of integrity who speaks the truth."

It is the final point in Paul's approach which is the most important: "My little children, of whom I travail in birth again until Christ be formed in you" (v. 19). He travailed in pain for them. He likened himself to a young mother. For nine months she has carried the child, she knows the agony of childbirth without anesthesia, and it is her first confinement. What a disappointment when the baby is stillborn. But because she loves and longs for a live child, she is prepared to go through it all again, to patiently bear the long months of suffering, to strive again in birth pangs, if only she may have the joy of bringing a live baby into the world. Paul had suffered physically, mentally, and spiritually for these Galatians. They had professed to believe in Christ, but there were no signs of new life. He was prepared to continue to suffer, to patiently plod on, to teach, to pray, if only spiritual life could be brought to at least some of them.

This is the outstanding lesson for all who labor among Muslim women and girls. Eternal life can only be brought to others when the servant is prepared to suffer in full fellowship with the

Saviour who died. These, then, are the principles which must guide you in your approach to Muslim women.

You must not expect to attract masses of Muslim women to your house or to your church. The Lord Jesus dealt with individuals. He talked to the woman at the well, to Mary who sat at His feet, to Mary as she wept at the tomb. He did not expect people to come to Him. He went to them. You must not expect these women to come to you, especially at the outset, but you must go to them. Jesus did speak at times to the crowds, but He certainly did not go to every house but instead concentrated on those who were attracted and interested. You must do this under the guidance of the Holy Spirit. You must look for open doors. When a woman has a baby, you can visit her with a little present for the child. Then you can chat with the mother. Perhaps before you leave you can suggest that you ask God's blessing on the little life. Never be tempted to admire the baby or say that it is pretty. Remember their abject fear of the "evil eye." Bereavement, divorce, and sickness can all provide an opportunity for a visit. Then you can suggest that you would like to return on some other occasion.

When you are allowed to enter a home, sit with the women on the mat. Take your shoes off to avoid treading on the mat on which they pray. If they sit on the floor, do not accept a chair but just sit as they do. Incidentally, you will find it an advantage not to have skirts that are too short! In any case, you must be prepared for an inspection of your underwear. They are often very inquisitive. Remember that even though you may still be young, you are a servant of God. Avoid outward display and loud boisterous laughter. A young worker can shock the women terribly in this way, especially if she laughs when men are about. They will ask you what your work is, and it is best to say quite plainly that you are a servant of God. "I am here among you because *God sent me* here to tell you things that you do not know." Never be tempted to say that a mission or a group has sent you. If you are not convinced that *God* has called and sent you, that He sustains and guides you each step of the way, then you had better stay at home.

This is really fundamental to your service. It is almost alarming to realize the extent to which the convert reflects the character of the missionary or leader. If you depend on your home group to send you out, to support you, and to sustain you by prayer, then the converts will reflect your attitude. They will depend on you and your group. If, on the other hand, you depend on the Lord alone for support, guidance, and strength, then right from the start you can teach them to be dependent on the Lord and not to count on you. Do not let them be your children, but cast them back on the Lord from the very beginning of their Christian life.

It is very important to direct them to a group of national believers or a local church as soon as possible. They will look to you to tell them what to do and what not to do, to give them a code of rules, because they have been reared in the atmosphere of Islam which is a legalistic religion. Give them *principles, not rules,* and let them work these out for themselves according to the background of their culture and country. Avoid introducing anything Western. It is always a tremendous help with Christians who have come out of Islam to make a careful and systematic study of the Galatian epistle. Such a study maintained over a period of weeks can effect a transformation in their spiritual life.

As you go on it is most important to:

Use your intelligence. Remembering that fear is the background of their lives, ask yourself just how you would react under the circumstances in which they live. Do not bring trouble on a woman by going against the customs of the land. Do not force yourself on a woman by knocking at her door when you are obviously not wanted. In fact, in some Muslim lands the very last thing to do is to knock at someone's door. Thus, you must learn the local customs. In my dispensary at the Hammam in Algeria I won the confidence of the population to such an extent that literally hundreds of veiled women would come for treatment. The veils came off and they would let me examine them thoroughly because they trusted me. But if I passed one of them in the street and she was closely veiled, I would give no sign of recognition. To have done so would have caused trouble for the woman. If a man is present in the house where a woman missionary is visiting, it usually will not be possible to speak to the women of spiritual things until he has left. In any case, it is usually best to wait for the mistress of the house to ask you to read the Bible to her. You are her guest, and she knows best. In so many ways you must know the people and exercise godly wisdom.

Use converts from Islam. They know their people better than any foreigner, and their advice will be invaluable. You may think they are overcautious, but you should weigh carefully anything that they say. Years of service have been wasted by missionaries who failed to take the advice of national Christians.

Use your senior missionaries. Again, you will need discernment. Observation should soon indicate whether a senior woman missionary has won the affection and confidence of the women. Length of service has nothing to do with this. There are many women workers (as well as men) who have spent years in a country without ever having been adopted by the people or ever having really entered into their life. Do not consult such persons. But where there are experienced senior missionaries who have an insight into the ways of the people, the younger missionary should ask for and follow their advice. This does not mean that you may not introduce any fresh avenues of approach, but be wise and use the advice of your fellow workers.

Use your eyes and ears. You will learn more in this way than in any other. The flicker of a smile will mean that you have made a bad mistake. It should be obvious if you have provoked resentment, anger, or pain by your words or actions. Then you must reflect and ask yourself where you have blundered. Ask yourself, "What have I said or done which has shocked them?" You will see them using sign language. While you are giving your message you will see them communicating to each other with their toes. Try and find out what it is they are saying. Learn their proverbs.

The women know many more of these than the men do, and it is a quick way to win their confidence. But be quite sure that there is no smutty meaning hidden in the proverb. You will have to learn to drink coffee from a cup which may not come up to your standard of cleanliness and to eat food that you would not even consider eating in your own home.

If you are asked, "What is your work?" you should immediately say that you are God's servant and that your job is to help others find the peace of God in their hearts. It is most important that you should be known *from the very outset* as a woman of the Book, and not as a nurse or a teacher, or even a missionary, just a woman of the Book. Then invitations will come to you to go to a shut-in woman and read to her from the Book. Someone else will drop in and in turn will be gripped by the message and ask you to her home. Remember that there is power in the Book. It is the weapon of the Holy Spirit.

Patience is needed more than anything else. Lalla Jouhra conducted a Bible class for women for a whole year with just one old woman attending. As the years went by, her class increased so that she often had twenty-five or thirty Muslim women each week, but she had only that one old woman for a year.

Girls who are studying at college in their own country or abroad like to convey the impression that they have broken with Islam. They attempt to copy Europeans, to be "with it." They may have abandoned the wearing of the veil, but that does not mean that they are open to Christianity. Yet, there are many among them who have a deep yearning to know God. These are the ones that you must seek. God knows them, and by His Holy Spirit He will lead you to them.

Finally, keep in mind these four things about Muslims:

1. They respond to love, real unaffected love. They know at once those who are transparently sincere in their love for God and for them.

2. They respond to their own language. Even though she may speak another language really well, if you speak to a woman in her own native tongue you will reach her heart.

3. They respond to prayer. Pray much for the Lord's wisdom and guidance before contacts, after a conversation, and continually.

4. They can only be won through suffering. You can only get to know a Muslim woman when you have won her confidence. Then she feels that she can trust you and will open up. This may take five years, or it may take twenty. Yet, once you have won this confidence, you are well on the way to winning the woman for your Lord. She often will trust the missionary more than one of her own race. But this trust must be won. It can be won by love and sympathy, but often it is by tears. Women's work is heartbreaking. As I won the confidence of teenage Muslim girls in successive camps in Algeria, put myself in their place, listened to their stories, and prayed for the right answer, my pillow was often wet with tears. It was not until I had wept over them that God used me to win some for Christ. They respond to tears. This is how you can win them for the Lord.

13

CONTROVERSY

The Christian should avoid controversy wherever possible, but he must never leave the impression that Muslim arguments against the Christian faith are conclusive and irrefutable. He must be prepared to face them and reply in love. He should always have before him the perfect Servant whose character is described in Isaiah 42:1-4. Paul had this passage in mind when he wrote to young Timothy: "The Lord's bond-servant must not be quarrelsome, but be kind to all . . . with gentleness correcting those who are in opposition" (2 Ti 2:24-25, NASB). *Learn this passage by heart.* Here are some helps:

1. *Avoid the attitude that provokes quarrels.* Say quite frankly, "I have not come to discuss religion, to debate, or to prove that Christianity is right. I just want to tell you something that you do not know." This will probably provoke a question such as this: "What is it that we do not know?" Your answer should be: "Do you know how to find peace with God? Do you know how to conquer Satan and the evil of your heart? I have found the answer to these questions and, if you will allow me, I want to share with you what I have found. Surely we can talk together and share what we believe."

2. *Avoid the subjects that provoke quarrels.* The inevitable choice for every Muslim man is Muhammad or Christ. Is the Bible right or the Koran? But it is useless to discuss the person of Muhammad or the value of the Koran. To do so is to provoke hostility. Our duty is to communicate the Good News, not to criticize their manner of praying, the conduct of their prophet, or the low morals of many Muslims. This only turns them away from the Lord.

3. *Avoid the places where you may provoke controversy.* In the early days of my ministry, I would often go to the mosque as the men gathered there. But the religious leaders are paid to defend Islam, so this was very unwise, for it led immediately into argument and a defense of my faith. On the other hand, in later years I was sometimes called into the mosque and asked to read from the Bible. In the country coffeehouses I found a much more neutral ground. Perhaps the very best place is in a friendly home, but it does take time to win their confidence and to gain entrance into a home.

What then should be your reply if asked, "What do you think of Muhammad?"

"If I did believe in him as you do, it is clear that I would not be a Christian."

"But why do you not believe in him? We believe in the Lord Jesus, why should you not in turn believe in our lord Muhammad?"

"Every believer seeks God's blessing. Can you show me a single blessing that I shall gain through believing in your prophet that I have not already found through faith in Christ?"

"What then do you think of Muhammad?"

In your reply you should always be courteous, giving some title to their prophet. You could point out: "Muhammad found the Arabs worshiping many gods and called them back to faith in one God. He established unity to a people torn by internal strife. There is much good that he did. He called himself a prophet sent from God, but he never claimed to be a savior. He claimed to be only a simple preacher. Jesus Christ claimed to be the Saviour from sin. Surely we can accept each one according to his claims. Muhammad showed men God's way by telling them not to sin, but Jesus Christ claimed to be the *only* way to God. Let us try and understand what each said about himself."

Or again, you could ask politely: "Where is Muhammad buried? Is it in Mecca or Medina? Where is the Lord Jesus? He is alive forevermore. He is risen from the dead. (Unless the Christian asks just where their prophet is buried, they will assert

that he is alive in the same way that Jesus is, only he is absent.)
How do I know that He lives? I have proof from the Scriptures
which I believe, but I also know because He lives within my
heart."

Remember that you can say almost anything to a Muslim if
you say it politely and with a smile. They know instinctively
when the Christian loves them, sympathizes with them, and longs
for their ultimate good.

Keep in mind that the Muslim may seek to provoke you and
make you lose your temper. He knows that if this happens,
others will no longer listen to you. On the other hand, if in a
group a man does lose his temper this can be turned to your
advantage. Stroking your beard or chin, say, "Please forgive me.
I had no intention of making you angry. If I had known you were
like that, I would not have told you the truth as forthrightly as I
did. Please forgive me." (A Turk's beard is said to bristle with
rage when he is cross.) Sometimes it is enough to stroke the
chin and look around at the others and smile.

If you are talking to a small group and a religious leader wants
to monopolize the conversation, it is wise to keep in mind the
other people and their spiritual needs. Speak for them and not
just to the man who wants to argue. Remember, they are watch-
ing you closely to see your reactions and are listening to you
intently.

There are times when one man in a group will continue to
oppose you. Take your watch and put it down in front of you,
saying, "I will give you ten minutes to tell us just what Muhammad has done for you. Then you must give me ten minutes to
tell you what Christ has done for me. I will listen while you
speak, and I trust you to do the same for me." Of course you
must be very polite and let him speak first! I have never known
a Muslim take more than two minutes before coming to a full
stop. Then you can tell from a full heart all that our wonderful
Lord means to you and to those of us who trust Him. If you do
not let the Muslim speak first, he will merely take all that you
have said about the Lord and apply it to Muhammad. This

method works well when a fanatical man is trying to monopolize the conversation in order to prevent others from hearing about the Lord.

It is almost inevitable at times, if you are working in villages or with groups of men, that one or more of them will be really annoyed. The only thing to do then is to leave them, while at the same time audibly invoking God's blessing on them. Perhaps they will curse you, but speak well of them and ask God's blessing on them. As soon as possible return to the group or to the village, not to recommence the discussion, but to show them that you still love them. Greet them in the usual way, sit with them, and chat. It is more than likely that you will find that they are really friendly and will ask questions about what you had tried to explain on the previous occasion. Love never fails.

Remember that a Muslim is always strong when he takes the offensive in a discussion. He fires a string of questions at you and puts you on the defensive; but if the role is reversed and you take the offensive, he is weak and perplexed. You will need very much love and tact to do this. You could say, "You claim that the Koran is the Word of God. Can you please give me a tangible proof of this?" Or again, "Jesus Christ has assured me of forgiveness for my past sins, hope for the future, and the peace of God now. What added blessing will be mine if I believe what you believe?"

Finally, it is very important to remember that the Holy Spirit, the Counselor, will guide you in all your answers. Count on Him to use your words as the sword of the Spirit. Above all, remember to pound in one nail at the time. Keep bringing the man back to the one subject, using the appropriate Scripture verses.

14

HELPING THE CONVERT

There is little doubt that the greatest need in the Muslim world today is for sympathetic workers who are able to put themselves in the place of Christians who were once Muslims, to appreciate their problems, to share their sufferings, and to make them feel that they are really understood and accepted by the other Christians. A tremendous gulf often separates the missionary in his comfortable home and modern car from the man who faces ostracism at every moment of the day, or the girl married to a Muslim. In Muslim lands the new Christian is literally faced with the loss of all things for Christ's sake. He often loses his home, his work, his position in the community, his status, his family, and sometimes even his life. Every day he meets ostracism, taunts, and sometimes blows. He is suspected as a traitor to his country. Rejected by one community, he is often regarded with suspicion by the Christians who are very reluctant to receive him into the local church.

It is most important that he should feel that the homes of Christians are open to him and that he will receive a welcome at any time, and that he will find someone with whom to share his problems and then pray with him. Here again the greatest lesson that the missionary can learn is the ability to listen until the whole story has been poured out.

A period of individual instruction should follow a profession of conversion. If the person is still young and cannot read, some effort should be made to teach him to read the Scriptures. If at all possible, he should be helped to read the Bible in his native tongue. The vast majority of young Christians in Muslim lands today read the New Testament in a European language simply because it is the only language which the missionary can speak or read fluently. The Classical Arabic Bible may be the answer, but in some lands young believers find it hard to follow, although they would usually be unwilling to admit this because it is good Arabic. If English is used, it is important to read a modern translation such as the New American Standard Bible.

It may well be that the convert has already learned sections of the Koran by heart. We must explain to him the difference between this and Bible study. His aim must not be to recite long passages but to regard the Bible as God's instructions to teach him how to live as a Christian. Through the Bible, God reveals His will. In contrast to the Koran which Muslims believe descended from heaven and was given to Muhammad by the angel Gabriel, the Bible was given over a long period of time with messages to suit the varying needs of many individuals. It is the inspired Word of God and is God's voice bringing God's message for every individual in whatever circumstances he may be living. He must look for Christ on every page of the Bible. He should find out what God says about how to live his everyday life. It is more than likely that the convert in the East will understand certain parts of the Bible far better than the missionary himself because the background of the Bible is that of his own Eastern country. Do not try and force your interpretation into any verse to make it fit in with evangelical doctrine. Take the New Testament at its face value.

The convert from Islam may have his Bible taken from him, be thrown into prison, or otherwise persecuted. Therefore he should be encouraged to memorize long passages so that he will be able to recall them in times of persecution. If he is able to listen to radio broadcasts, this will help him realize that he is a member of a large worldwide family. He should be encouraged to follow a system of daily Bible reading such as that published by Scripture Union.

This passage in Acts 2:41-42 (NASB) should be brought to his notice soon after conversion: "Those who had received his word were *baptized.* . . . And they were continually devoting themselves to the *apostles' teaching* and to *fellowship,* to the *breaking of bread* and to *prayers."*

BAPTISM

Baptism is generally regarded by Muslims as the decisive break with Islam because it constitutes an open profession of faith in Christ. It is very doubtful if anyone can really remain a "secret believer" and never confess his faith. To continually hide his light and to live a double life is to lose his joy in the Lord. The first step then is to confess Christ, to own him as Lord by telling others in and outside the home of the wonderful change that He has brought about. Before taking the next step of baptism, several things must be considered. Baptism is usually followed by admission to church membership and the partaking of the Lord's Supper. Most Christians think that it is dishonoring to the Lord to abstain from partaking of the Lord's Supper because a man is observing the Muslim fast of Ramadan. The Christian must be reminded of this. It will cost him a lot to break the fast, thus the willingness to do so and to be baptized should leave little doubt that he is a sincere believer. This being so, he should not be required to wait for baptism for a long period after his conversion as is the case in some pagan countries. This is usually to ascertain the reality of the convert's new life in Christ. The convert from Islam is willing to face death itself to prove his sincerity, so it should be obvious that if he really desires baptism and realizes all the implications of this act of obedience and identification with his Lord, he should not be compelled to wait. In the case of a minor, permission must be obtained from his parents. A young woman who has become a Christian can scarcely be baptized without the permission of her husband and probably her parents. Great care must be taken to shield her in every possible way and to ensure her protection.

Some believers may want to postpone baptism until they are in a position to be virtually independent of the society in which they live. If it is possible to baptize several persons at one time, this would be ideal.

THE APOSTLES' TEACHING

Every effort should be made to give regular instruction in all the fundamental truths of the New Testament. Galatians is an ideal book for those who have come to Christ from Islam. If collective studies cannot be arranged, then individual teaching is essential. The new convert must be able to explain his faith to others and to meet their objections from the New Testament. For instance, his Muslim friend may insist that Jesus foretold the coming of Muhammad. He must be able to point him to John 14:16 (NASB): "I will ask the Father, and He will give you another Helper." "Yes, that is it," the Muslim will assert. The Christian must point his Muslim friend to the context, emphasizing "that He may be with you forever." Then he should ask: "Is he still with you?" The next verse shows just who the helper is: "That is, the Spirit of truth." He must be taught to use the Word, the sword of the Spirit, first on himself, and then in defense of his newfound faith.

FELLOWSHIP

Fellowship is what the young Christian needs more than anything else in Muslim lands. While he was a Muslim he formed part of a vast community, in which he was accepted. Now that he is a Christian, he shows at every moment of the day that he is one apart, for Islam enters into every aspect of everyday life. It is most important that local Christians surround him with love and care so that he feels he belongs. This is even more important than special doctrines and beliefs. He is now cut off from the old community. He must feel that he really belongs to the new one. There must be an atmosphere of love in the church.

He will feel very strange in church gatherings at first. It is important to try to look at them through his eyes. In the mosque there was a sense of reverence and awe. He will expect to find this in the church, but often it is lacking in evangelical circles. Islam is characterized by the prominence that it gives to praise and worship. Thank God this is growing among younger Christians today as the Holy Spirit is acknowledged and allowed to control them. The messages should always be straightforward, relevant to his everyday needs, and given in love.

BREAKING OF BREAD

The breaking of bread is something that the new convert from Islam can really enter into, as it approaches in some way the ritual of Islam. It is something that he can do to show his love for the Lord Jesus as he remembers Him and comes to His table to meet Him. Before he is received into church membership it should be pointed out that to partake of the Lord's Supper involves breaking away from Islam, especially during the fast of Ramadān.

PRAYERS

We have seen that in Islam, prayer is a ritual performed at stated times, and always in Arabic. The new Christian will probably miss this, and it will take some time for him to understand that when the Christian prays he is talking to his heavenly Father. He should certainly be taught the model prayer of Matthew 6:9-13, for this should form the basis for his daily prayers. His chief difficulty will be to find a place where he can be alone with his Father to pray and meditate on His Word. It is virtually impossible in a Muslim home to be quiet and alone with God. If he is a man, he will be able to get away into the fields or mountains. Some women have to make their own prayer closet by pulling a blanket over their heads at night. Although he is in the habit of saying "In the name of God" before his meals, he must be taught that the Christian thanks God for everything, including his food. Teach him to thank God for the spiritual blessings which he has received in Christ. It will help him to learn to model his prayers on this pattern: "Thank You, Lord. Forgive me, Lord. Please, Lord." He should pour out his heart in thanksgiving, confessing anything which has come in to hinder his communion with God and asking forgiveness, and then interceding for himself and others, asking for definite answers in the name of Christ.

It may be of help to try to put yourself in the place of Christians in Muslim lands. Remember all that they give up for the Lord's sake. To leave Islam is to become an apostate, to be regarded as a traitor to his country, to face continued opposition and persecution from the religious authorities, the civil authorities, and most of all, from his own family. With this in mind, the foreigner will do all in his power to shield the convert. And in his efforts at outreach, he will always bear in mind the reactions that his rash yet zealous actions may have on local Christians. The foreigner can leave the country after his misguided blunders, but the national Christian must remain and pay the price. It is here that we show how deep and sincere is our love for the Lord and others. May God save us from being immature and superficial Christians in this realm.

15

FINAL SUGGESTIONS AND CONCLUSION

1. Muslims are often critical of European dress, but to wear a tarboush or a headscarf as Muslim women do in most Muslim lands is to be immediately classified as having accepted Islam. Naturally it is difficult to make a statement that covers all countries. Women and girls living in the country should be consulted. The reply of a university student obviously will differ from that of a poorer woman, but all must be taken into consideration. In Algeria the expression *the shoudd thimharemth* (she has put on a headscarf) means that the person has become a Muslim. The male missionary should not wear shorts when going to Muslims, and the girl who wears short skirts will be very embarrassed when sitting on mats with Muslim women. As much of the body as possible should be covered. This does not apply so much in Central Africa among Islamized pagans as it does in the Middle East.

2. In attempting village work with Muslims, the most important point is to choose carefully your seat and position. You must have all your audience in front of you, where you can see them and control them with your eyes. To sit with a critical Muslim behind you, or in a two-story building with someone overhead who is opposed, is fatal. There will be no need for the other man even to speak. He can use signs and mimic to decry all that you say.

3. If it can be avoided, it is unwise to talk to a Muslim about his personal faith or about your own faith in the presence of others. He will immediately think that he must defend or promote his religion. If at all possible, speak to him alone. This

91

also applies to countries where part of the population is Muslim and part pagan or Christian.

4. In Muslim evangelization it is wise to follow the Master's orders and go out two by two. There is no possible advantage in going as a band and there are many disadvantages.

5. When going to Muslims who sit on mats, do not hesitate to sit with them. They may bring a chair and want you to sit there as a sort of chief, but this must be avoided at all costs. Let them see that you are just as human as they are and that you want to share, not dominate. Remember that they use their mats for prayer and for this reason they remove their shoes before walking on a mat. The missionary should do the same. It is merely being polite.

6. It will be noticed that usually a teacher sits to speak. In this the worker should conform to local practice. In most Muslim countries it is best not to stand and preach, but to sit. There are exceptions, and sometimes one has to stand to preach in a market, if this is possible and permitted. Where open-air meetings are prohibited by the law of the land, the Christian must be law-abiding.

7. It is most important to read from the Bible and to let the people see that it is in their language, especially if it is in Arabic characters. Arabic is called the "tongue of the angels," and they almost show reverence to the Arabic script. We can make use of this superstition by showing that we, too, admire it and take pleasure in reading it.

8. With Muslims it is wise to give a simple direct message lasting for approximately ten minutes. This initial message should form the focal point of the conversation, and the missionary should revert to it continually during the discussion. Before leaving the group, the outstanding points should be emphasized again.

9. Deal with one subject at a time. If speaking on repentance, deal thoroughly with that aspect of truth. Do not mix up messages on forgiveness and peace and eternal life, etc. One truth at a time is sufficient.

10. Never be afraid to speak the whole truth. The Muslim admires the man who courageously says what he believes.

11. If you are asked a question to which you do not know the answer, it is best to say so. Promise that you will think over the matter and will let the person know the answer at some future time.

12. Remember that a fundamental rule of teaching is to start with the truth which they know and to proceed to fresh truth.

13. Pray before going out to Muslims, and when you have left them.

14. Each time prepare a definite message and have notes in your Bible written in the language of the people. Underline the verses or verse which is to be the keynote of the talk. Have all important verses marked in your Bible so that you can find them easily.

15. Depend on the Holy Spirit to lead you. You may not be led to give the message you have prepared, but no doubt it will be useful at some other time.

16. Keep a book in which you note all their objections to the Christian faith. Keep one page for each objection. Pray quietly about each one. Ask God to show you what Scripture verses deal effectively with that objection. Think through any illustration that you can use. In what way can you explain the Christian faith so that you remove a particular difficulty from the Muslim's mind?

17. It is wisest to avoid doctrines which are not specifically dealt with in a passage of Scripture, for instance, the doctrine of the Trinity. Illustrations such as the same man acting in three capacities as a church member, husband, and baker do not impress a Muslim. Nor does that of the sun which is seen as a celestial body, can be seen as sunshine, and in whose rays you can bask. These may convince a Western mind, but they fail to convey truth to a Muslim.

18. Remember that until a man is convicted that he is a sinner he will never seek a Saviour. He will never truly repent unless he sees sin as rebellion against God. He will never bow to Christ as

Lord apart from the Holy Spirit. We are utterly dependent upon Him.

19. The Muslim is singularly unimpressed by the Christian who speaks in tongues. He will attribute this to evil spirits or call the Christian a *dervish*. The Muslim fails to understand that a man can claim to speak in tongues and yet be incapable of learning the Muslim's dialect or language. The best proof to him of the power of the Holy Spirit is a message which is relevant to his need, spoken in his own tongue, and based on the Bible. He will invariably be attracted and want to hear more.

20. Remember the importance of the Bible. A message may be quickly forgotten, but the Scriptures speak continually. Widespread free distribution of Scripture portions is most unwise. It is far better to sell the New Testament or gospels than to give them away. A Muslim appreciates something that he has to buy. He may well refuse to buy it because it does not have the Muslim formula *bi ism Allah* written or printed on it. Remind him that when he purchases bread it does not have *bi ism Allah* on it. He says *bi ism Allah* and eats, so why not do the same with the bread of life, the Word of God?

Remember to treat the Bible with the same reverence as they treat the Koran. They will never hold the Koran lower than the waistline because it is precious and holy to them. For this reason when they see tracts or Scriptures which contain the name of God trampled underfoot, they tend to despise them. Thus, much wisdom is needed to make the Bible or some portion of it available, yet not to distribute it in such a way as to lower its value in the eyes of the people. We are the people of the Book. May we revere it and honor it as the Word of the living God.

It is evident today that God is working among the Muslims of many lands. Many are seeking the truth. Numbers are trusting the Saviour and facing ostracism, persecution, and even death with tremendous courage. As doors in some lands close, the Lord is calling more young people to serve Him among Muslims. The evangelization of Muslims requires much patience, but it is very rewarding and brings glory to God. The Lord's will is that *every* man and woman should hear the Good News. Let us work on until that day when a great multitude which no man could number, from every nation, from all tribes and peoples and tongues stand before the throne, crying with a loud voice, "Salvation to our God who sits on the throne, and to the Lamb" (Rev 7:10, NASB).